Anonymous

Letters to a Young Nobleman

Anonymous

Letters to a Young Nobleman

ISBN/EAN: 9783337779931

Printed in Europe, USA, Canada, Australia, Japan

Cover: Foto ©Thomas Meinert / pixelio.de

More available books at **www.hansebooks.com**

LETTERS

TO A

Young Nobleman.

CIVIS ET EGREGIUS PATRIÆ CONTINGÍS OVANTI.

LONDON:
Printed for A. MILLAR, in the Strand.
MDCCLXII.

CONTENTS.

Letter		Page.
I.	On Study in general,	1
II.	On the Study of History,	7
III.	On the same subject,	21
IV.	On Biography,	53
V.	Of Taste; and of some distinguishing circumstances of London and Paris,	75
VI.	On the Influence of Liberty upon Taste; and of the Age of Augustus,	96
VII.	On the Influence of Liberty upon Taste; and of the Age of Lewis XIV,	153
VIII.	Why Poetry has flourished more in England than Sculpture or Painting,	197

LETTERS

TO A

Young Nobleman.

LETTER I.

On Study in general.

My Lord,

YOUR Lordship's high rank and quality, your fortune and prospects in the world, will make abundance of people desirous of your company, fond of appearing with you at public places, and of being of your parties at every gay scene of diversion, pleasure and amusement. Allow me, my Lord, to have another ambition, and to make use of that correspondence you have desired me to trouble you with, to become the companion of your most private hours and least dissipated moments.

I HOPE your Lordship has a great many such hours; for, though you are now entering

ing upon that period of life, which none, but surly, morose, and foolish pedants, would debar from gaiety and diversion, yet upon the manner in which you employ your present time, does your future figure and character in the world depend. As well might a husbandman, who should be altogether idle in seed-time, expect to reap a plentiful crop, as one who trifles away the spring of his life, in foolish dissipation or vitious riot, to attain to honour and renown, or to acquire the character of a wise and great man.

Look around you, my Lord, and observe who have attained to a high reputation for wisdom and abilities, then enquire how they spent their youth: turn over the annals of history, mark the names which have been transmitted down to posterity with honour and applause, read the list of patriots and heroes, study their lives, and you will find that their behaviour during their youth, when they were preparing themselves for appearing upon the theatre of the world, laid the foundation of whatever figure they made,

or

or whatever glory they acquired, when they came to act their different parts in life.

'Tis the duty of all young people, my Lord, to improve their minds, and to fit themselves for the world; but in a particular manner, 'tis the duty of young noblemen, as upon their characters much depends, and they have many helps and advantages which those of inferior rank are deprived of. Others must labour to acquire knowledge and skill in those different professions by which they propose to make their fortunes in the world; their thoughts must be principally employed about particular details; only a part of their time, and sometimes a very small part of it, can be spared to study what may improve them in a general knowledge of men and manners, and in a graceful and easy politeness. But those, whom fortune has placed in such circumstances as your Lordship's, have all the time they could wish for, to make themselves accomplished gentlemen.

Besides, my Lord, the paths of knowledge, your ſtation calls upon you to purſue, are not rugged, dull, or diſagreeable; on the contrary, they are the moſt ſmooth, chearful and entertaining imaginable. To read the works of thoſe immortal authors, who have expreſſed the nobleſt ſentiments in the fineſt language; to ſtudy the hiſtory of mankind, and to become acquainted with what has happened in the different countries and ages of the world; to obſerve the gradual riſe and decline of arts and ſciences, to reflect upon their cauſes, to ſtudy the conſtitution of your country, and to conſider what alterations have happened in it, and how theſe have been brought about; what is there in all this that does not promiſe the higheſt entertainment? The lawyer muſt ſlave many years in reading reports and acts of parliament; the phyſician muſt ſpend much time in fixing in his memory the names and properties of medicines, and in ſtudying the mechaniſm of the different parts of the human body; in every profeſſion much inſipid drudgery muſt be undergone, before one can

can possibly expect to become eminent. But to arrive at that knowledge, which is necessary to make a man of rank and fortune useful in the world, happy and agreeable in himself, a support and delight to his friends, a guardian and ornament to his country, no such drudgery is necessary. He can hardly ever employ his time in a manner proper for his improvement, without spending it in such a way as must afford him more real pleasure, even when he is alone and busy, than any idle trifler can possibly enjoy in his irrational and foolish parties of dissipation.

I was just going to say, that if the ways which would lead a young man of quality to honour and glory be so easy and agreeable, how inexcusable must their folly be who widely wander from the enlightened road of wisdom, to follow the dark paths of ignorance, which lead to infamy and reproach. But, my Lord, when I reflect upon your Lordship's good dispositions, methinks I have already said too much, and that I ought to make an apology for what I have written.

LETTER I.

IF my correspondence can be any way agreeable to you, much more if it can be useful, I shall reckon myself extremely happy, and shall omit no opportunity of communicating my thoughts to you, whenever it appears to me, that they may possibly be of any advantage, or afford entertainment to your Lordship.

I am, &c.

LETTER II.

On the STUDY of HISTORY.

MY LORD,

SOME knowledge of history is expected of every one, who pretends to a character above that of the meanest vulgar. Of those indeed whom fortune has,

------ Doom'd to scythes and spades,
And all those hard laborious trades *;

And whose situation in life affords them no opportunities of instruction, a knowledge of any thing beyond the bounds of their own narrow circle is not expected. But they, to whom fortune has been more liberal, whose

* Fable of the Bees.

spirits are not oppressed by corporeal labour, and who have leisure to open the fair book of knowledge, hardly deserve the name of men, if, satisfied with every trifling incident that occurs to them in their own little sphere of action, their curiosity never prompts them to enquire what has been done in ages and countries different from their own; or to review those great events which have happened on this terrestrial globe in its various periods. The age of man, if extended to its utmost duration, is but a very confined period, and so much of it passes away in the thoughtless play-time of infancy, so much of it is swallowed up by the violent passions of youth, so much of it is entirely lost in sleep and necessary rest; that the remaining part, even though we were to suppose every moment employed in reflection and observation, must be reduced to a very small point. That knowledge, therefore, which is derived from personal experience alone, must be confined within very narrow limits. Hence the utility of history is obvious, which by carrying us back through a chain of events, to that

æra

æra when truth is loſt in fable, lengthens out, as it were, the period of human life; and puts us in poſſeſſion of obſervations drawn from the experience of ſucceſſive ages*. I do not mean to inſinuate however, that the trueſt wiſdom is not the fruit of experience, but only that the beſt method of enabling us to make juſt reflections, and to draw true conclusions from what happens to ourſelves, or falls within our own obſervation, is to become acquainted with what has happened to others, and with what their conduct has been in circumſtances ſimilar to our own.

WE muſt often, my Lord, find ourſelves, eſpecially at our ſetting out in life, in ſituations new to us, and quite different from any thing we have experienced before; thoſe, therefore, who are uninſtructed how others have

---

* Nec enim ſuam tantum ætatem bene tuentur: omne ævum ſuo adjiciunt. Quicquid annorum ante illos actum eſt, illis acquiſitum eſt——nullo nobis ſæculo interdictum eſt: in omnia admittimur; et ſi magnitudine animi egredi humanæ imbecillitatis anguſtias libet, multum per quod ſpatiemur temporis eſt.

SENEC.

acted

acted in such circumstances, must be blest with uncommon judgment and quickness, not to be liable to fall into errors, and sometimes into such errors, as may have a fatal influence upon their future conduct.

Many examples might be brought to prove, that the Study of History may in some measure supply the want of experience. Allow me to put you in mind of the known story of Lucullus; who, though he went from Rome, ignorant of the art of war, yet by spending the time of his journey and voyage partly in asking questions of men of knowledge, and partly in reading the History of former actions*, came to Asia with such a character, and performed such exploits as obliged the great Mithridates to confess, that he had found him to be an abler general than any of those concerning whom he had read †. The example, I own,

---

* Partim in percunctando a peritis, partim in rebus gestis legendis.

† Hunc a se majorem ducem cognitum, quam quenquam eorum quos legisset.

is trite; but it is taken from an author who cannot be too often quoted; and I am perfuaded your Lordſhip will review the whole paſſage, at the beginning of the ſecond Book of Tully's Academical Queſtions, with a great deal of pleaſure.

To this I might add a numerous liſt of other examples, but I am perfuaded you are already convinced how much a careful and judicious ſtudy of the conduct of others, as exhibited in hiſtory, may enable us to act in a proper manner: permit me only to mention one modern, as I did one antient example of this truth; does not Europe at preſent, with admiration, behold the conduct of a great prince and general, who prepared himſelf for illuſtrious actions by indefatigable ſtudy, particularly of hiſtory; and hath even ſhewn, that as he can perform actions which will for ever make a figure in the annals of mankind, ſo he can relate * thoſe which were performed by others, in a truly maſterly manner?

* Memoires de Branden.

LETTER II.

BEGINNING to act our parts in life, without enquiring how others have trode the stage before us, is as absurd, as to travel to a foreign country without knowing any thing of the language or manners of the people whom we are to visit, and will expose us to as many improprieties of conduct, and errors in judgment. How much quicker must his improvement be, and with how much greater certainty and facility must he make observations about any country, who is acquainted with its language, geography, customs and history, than he who sets out unskilled, and ignorant of all these things? Your Lordship will readily agree with me that the difference must be great; just such a difference is there between him who ventures to act his part in the world, ignorant of every thing that has happened before him, and one who has joined to a knowledge of arts and sciences, a knowledge of history, of the most remarkable actions which men have performed, of the characters of those who performed them, of the springs which gave rise to

On the STUDY of HISTORY.

to thofe actions, and of the confequences which were derived from them, either to the actors themfelves, to their country, or to the world.

I obferved before, that fome knowledge of Hiftory is expected from every one who is of a rank above that of the loweft mechanic, but it is not neceffary for every one, who is above that rank, to be equally well acquainted with it. Some may read the tranfactions of former ages, to entertain and unbend their minds, after a ftudious application to the proper bufinefs of their different profeffions; fome may do it to amufe themfelves, and to acquire fuch a fhare of knowledge as may make them entertaining companions, and fit them for the converfation of men of fenfe and learning. But, my Lord, you will be convinced that Hiftory is the proper ftudy of a nobleman, if you reflect that it is principally taken up in relating great actions, or the actions of great men.

LETTER II.

THE chief subjects of History, are such events as peculiarly intereſt the ſuperior part of mankind, and in producing or preventing which, their ſtation obliges them to have ſome ſhare. The riſe and fall of kingdoms and ſtates, the eſtabliſhment of liberty and laws, or the encroachments of ſlavery and deſpotiſm, the flouriſhing of arts and ſciences, or the prevalence of ignorance and barbarity; the enervating effects of luxury and vice, or the happy influence of temperance and virtue: Theſe, my Lord, are the contents of the hiſtoric page, and in theſe men of quality and fortune are deeply intereſted, as their conduct muſt neceſſarily have great influence in promoting the grandeur and happineſs, or preventing the fall and miſery of their country. A man of fortune and rank cannot poſſibly be an idle ſpectator of human affairs; one way or other he muſt do good or harm. He can never be ſo retired as not to have ſome influence; and indeed when he wholly abſtracts himſelf, and becomes entirely regardleſs how affairs are managed, he not only acts a mean, but in ſome measure,

measure, a criminal part, as every nobleman is born to take a share in governing the world, and by becoming quite careless of its concerns, he, as it were, forsakes and neglects that post, which it was his duty to watch and guard.

Is then history chiefly relates such actions, as the first men of a country have had, and must have, a principal share in; when a young nobleman is reading history, tracing back the great events and revolutions of human affairs to their springs and causes, considering the characters of legislators and heroes, and comparing what they did with their various methods of acting, he is as much busied and employed in studying his own profession, as a watchmaker, who is viewing the machinery of a clock, and considering its springs and movements; or an anatomist, who is dissecting a human body, and observing the use of all its parts, and how they produce those effects for which nature intended them; a knowledge of the individual human frame is not more the anatomist's business, than that of the

the whole complex political body of mankind is the bufinefs, and ought to be the ftudy of every one who is born to a fuperior rank in any country; but chiefly, my Lord, in a free country, where all authority does not center in one perfon, but where every member of the commonwealth has fome influence according to his rank; thofe of your quality are born to be fenators, counfellors, and guardians of the dignities and prerogatives of the fovereign, and of the privileges of the people. In fuch a country, and fuch a one is Great Britain, 'tis more efpecially the duty of a nobleman to ftudy Hiftory, as by it alone, he can learn how tyrants have endeavoured to fap the foundations of liberty; by what methods they have attempted to enflave their fubjects, and by what means fubjects have been enabled to refift their lawlefs attempts, to fecure their own freedom, and fix their rights upon more determinate and lafting foundations.

WHENCE, but from the ftudy of Hiftory, can your Lordfhip acquire fuch a fund of know-

knowledge as will enable you to be an instructive and perfuasive speaker in the British senate? 'Tis a common opinion that we must be born poets, but that we may become orators; " nascimur poetæ, fimus oratores." And undoubtedly though to become a perfect orator, one must be endued by nature with a genius superior to that of the bulk of men, yet pains and industry may make any one of a good judgment and ordinary imagination a tolerable speaker, especially if he begins to improve himself when young: and how can this be better done than by making ourselves masters of the great events, and of the principal characters, which are handed down to us in history. This is one of those ways by which one may become an orator, and lay in such a store of knowledge, as will be ready at hand almost on all occasions. " Condo et " compono quæ mox depromere possim."---- may with great propriety be applied by a young nobleman to himself, when he is employed in studying History.

LETTER II.

IF one makes himself master of his subject, and has his mind stocked with ideas proper to be brought out, it will not be found so difficult, as some may imagine, to express them in a proper manner: for as Horace, whom I beg leave to quote once more to you, has it, verba---prævisam rem haud invita se-
" quentur; which may surely as well be said of a public speaker, as of a poet.

BUT History will not only furnish you with the best materials and ground-work of public speaking; it will also present you with the noblest models: not even the rapid oratory of Demosthenes, nor that flowing eloquence which charms us in Tully's Orations, exceed some of those speeches which we find in Livy, Salust, and other historians. Besides, those fine speeches, which we meet with when reading History, have this additional advantage, that we come to read them at a time, when the historian has interested us in those events which gave rise to them, and when our imaginations are warmed, and receive a deeper

im-

impreffion. Thus, being more ſtruck, we remember them better, and remember them too in ſuch a way, that we can eaſily make uſe of them on a proper occaſion; for the hiſtorical narration making us acquainted with the events of the times, and the oration being a ſort of commentary upon the facts and circumſtances of the hiſtory, they mutually throw light upon each other, and enable us to form a more certain judgment of the ſubject we are confidering.

'Tis not only in claſſic hiſtories that we meet with excellent ſpeeches, even modern hiſtory will preſent you with ſuch as will delight and inſtruct you; but chiefly in the hiſtory of your own country you will find, both in its remote and latter periods, ſuch ſpeeches as neither Greece nor Rome would have had any reaſon to have been aſhamed of. Liberty, my Lord, is an animating ſubject; and as it has warmed the breaſt of many Britiſh ſenators, ſo what they have ſpoke in the cauſe of freedom has ſtirred up the patriot flame in the boſoms of others, and in-

ſpired

spired them to purfue the beft meafures in fupport of the honour of their king, and the welfare of their country.

Thus, my Lord, a young nobleman has every motive to ftudy Hiftory: his own amufement, the good of his country, and what has always great influence with a virtuous mind, the applaufe of his countrymen, by being an ornament to his own rank, a wife counfellor to his king, and an able guardian of the rights of the people.

I am, &c.

LETTER III.

On the STUDY of HISTORY.

MY LORD,

MEN are so much the same in all ages, and in all countries, that the history of whatever nation you read, will afford you some opportunities of comparing what happened there, with what has been transacted in your own country, and of forming proper principles for the regulation of your future conduct: though the nearer the constitution, climate, and situation of the people, whose history you read, approach to the circumstances of your own country, the more ample field will there be for drawing comparisons, and for making useful and interesting observations.

LETTER III.

BEFORE one begins to study the history of any particular nation in the detail, a general idea of the history of mankind at large ought to be acquired. This opens the mind, removes prejudices, and convinces us how ill founded those extravagant ideas are, which most young people are apt to entertain of the superior grandeur and consequence of their own times, and of that part of the world in which their own country is situated.

WHEN your Lordship views in history the mighty actions of the great Empires which flourished in the most remote periods of antiquity, you will be astonished at the grandeur and virtue of the antients, and be almost tempted to look down with contempt upon the littleness of modern times. There is nothing tends more to enlarge our ideas, than a view of the magnificence of the antient world: the nearer we approach to that period, when men were first placed on this earth to be its principal inhabitants, the more striking pictures do we meet with of that grand sim-

simplicity, which is the characteristic of the primitive ages of the world.

THE first, the most venerable, and sacred of all books, gives us the noblest representations of the native simplicity of the original fathers of the human race. This informs us, and all other histories confirm the truth, that men and empires first appeared in the east. Here flourished those heroes and demi-gods of whom the antients have said so much, and with whose exploits one would choose to be acquainted, was it for no other reason, but that we might be able to read the antient poets with taste, and to distinguish the ingenious remains of antient art. This, we must be altogether unable to do, without a competent knowledge of the history of those fabulous and heroic ages; from which painters and statuaries have been supplied with the most beautiful, and the greatest number of the subjects that have employed their various talents, and which are the foundation of the noblest paintings, and most exquisite statues that adorn the world, and are the admiration all good judges of the fine arts. A gentleman who should seem to know little about the subjects whence these are taken, would make but a poor figure, and have no great reason to value himself upon having had a liberal education.

Besides, there is something grand and pleasing in the stories of those fabulous times: the labours of Hercules, Theseus and Jason, the justice of Minos and Radamanthus, and the various atchievements of so many others, please the mind, and amply repay that small portion of time which is spent in becoming tolerably well acquainted with their stories. For, to spend a deal of time in grammatical and critical researches concerning their genealogies, and the disputable parts of their history, is perhaps a wasting of time in any one; but would be much more so in a young nobleman, than in a professed grammarian or antiquary.

The great empires which flourished in the east, the Egyptian, the Assyrian, the Babylonian,

Ionian, and the Perſian, will undoubtedly claim your attention, afford you much amuſement, and ſurprize you with the accounts of many of thoſe great exploits, which their kings and princes performed, of the great works which they executed, and of thoſe ſtupendous monuments which they erected, and which ſtill remain to be the wonder of our times, and amazing proofs of what great undertakings the antients were capable of attempting and finiſhing.

But whatever amuſement and inſtruction the hiſtory of thoſe eaſtern empires may afford you, and however proper it be, that you ſhould become ſomewhat acquainted with their hiſtory, it would be far from being ſo, that you ſhould ſpend as much time and dwell as long upon it, as upon that of other nations, which will afford you far more inſtruction, and the circumſtances of whoſe affairs will appear far more intereſting to a Britiſh nobleman: for, leaving thoſe eaſtern countries behind you, and following arts and ſciences in their courſe weſtward, you will naturally come

come to Greece, a country, which though of no great extent, compared to those vast empires, yet, under the auspicious influence of freedom, made far greater improvements in arts and sciences, and civil life.

The history of Greece claims your attention on many accounts: one may with great propriety address to young noblemen of your rank, that advice which Horace gives in his art of poetry,

--------Vos exemplaria Græca
Nocturna versate manu, versate diurna.

The Greeks were a free people, and among them we find models of governments inclining to all the different kinds, Monarchy, Aristocracy, and Democracy. You will see what tended to preserve these constitutions in their first purity, what tended to overturn them, and at last bring ruin upon the whole country: you will have various occasions of applying what happened in Greece to what has happened, or may happpen, in Great
Britain:

Britain: for though none of their governments was exactly the same with ours, yet in all countries, where liberty prevails, there are so many resemblances and similar circumstances, that the history of one free country becomes peculiarly interesting to the inhabitants of another, especially to such of them, as by their station are called upon to have some share in the government.

BESIDES, that liberty which flourished in Greece, inspired the people with a quickness, elegance and vigour of genius, more than has yet appeared in any other nation. Thus not only their statesmen and warriors acted with wisdom and vigour, but their philosophers reasoned acutely, their poets were inspired with a truly poetic spirit, their artists executed with genius and elegance, and their historians narrated the actions of their countrymen in the noblest manner.

THE history of Greece, therefore, is particularly instructive and agreeable, not only on on account of the events which are the subject of it, but also the manner in which those events are narrated. When we read the best Grecian Historians, the writer's art makes us fancy we are acquainted with the persons whose characters he draws; and the power of imagination carries us back, and makes us, as if we were members of some one of the Grecian states, become interested in its affairs, anxious for the fate of a battle, and concerned for the effect which the harangues of some of their orators shall have upon the assembly of the people.

And here, my Lord, allow me to make this observation, that to be conversant in the History of those free states, to know how their affairs were managed, and how their popular assemblies were influenced, is, as it were, being acquainted with business, and transacting affairs in theory and speculation, before one comes to be concerned in such matters in life and practice: on which account a study of the Grecian and Roman Histories, which commonly go hand in hand,
ought

ought very juftly to make, as they generally do, a confiderable part of a young nobleman's education.

The Hiftory of the Roman people is full of the moft interefting and furprizing events, that are exhibited to us in the annals of human kind; whether we confider their fmall and inconfiderable beginnings, or the extenfive Empire to which they at laft attained; whether we confider the internal conftitution, of their government, or the mighty provinces they fubdued, and the manner in which they civilized and incorporated them with the main body of the Empire. No Hiftory is more fertile in grand events, or prefents us with greater examples of bravery, patriotifm, and integrity of manners, or of wifdom in debate, manly eloquence and confummate art in managing the heads, and influencing the hearts of a free people.

The Romans too have produced a number of writers, who in the nobleft manner have tranfmitted down to pofterity the wife conduct

duct and brave exploits of their renowned countrymen. There are two or three of their Historians, who alone, if studied judiciously, and with a true spirit of making observations, might furnish out an excellent system of political knowledge, and afford examples of almost every thing that can happen in such a country as Great Britain. Livy, Salust, Tacitus, authors, who, though they write in very different manners, are yet each of them excellent in their own way, and have been the delight and admiration of all good judges from their own, down to our times, and will continue to be so, while genius and letters are cultivated among men.

WHETHER the Grecian or the Roman Historians are the best, is perhaps doubtful, and is certainly immaterial to be determined. Quintilian, one of the most masterly critics who ever wrote, is of opinion, that his countrymen, in writing history, were not inferior to the Greeks *, and that one need not be afraid to oppose Salust to Thucydides, and Livy to

* Historiâ non cesserit Græcis.

Hero-

On the Study of History. 31

Herodotus. No Historian is more worthy of your study than Livy: the grandeur of his subject, the length of that period of time which his narration comprehends, the richness *, the beauty and purity of his style, his art in interesting and moving the affections and passions, and that admirable eloquence with which he transmits to us the principal of those orations which were spoken, or which he supposes were so, on the most remarkable occasions, which occur in the course of his narration, make every one of taste agree with the critic whom I just now mentioned, in allowing him to be eloquent in his speeches beyond expression †, and recommend him as one of the best authors for a young nobleman to study, and make himself thoroughly master of.

The comprehensive brevity of Salust, those sententious observations and moral maxims with which he intersperses his writings, and

* Livii lactea ubertas. *Quint.*
† In concionibus supra quam narrari potest eloquentem.

which

which render them peculiarly animated and instructing, cannot fail of making us highly value those precious remains which we have of him, and regret that the greatest part of his works is lost. Every line of him that we have entire, affords matter for reflection, and the oftner you read him, the more you will be persuaded that his writings, which unfortunately are so small, contain a vast fund of entertainment and instruction.

We may very properly characterise Tacitus, one of the deepest geniuses that ever appeared among men, by these lines in which Shakespear describes Cassius.

> He is a great observer; and he looks
> Quite through the deeds of men----
> Seldom he smiles------

Seldom indeed does he present to us the smiling side; but often exposes to our view the dark and gloomy shades of that picture which he draws of human affairs; like the Duke de la Rochefoucault, who is known to have been a great admirer of him, he is by many people thought too fevere in his cenfures, and too apt to attribute actions to bad motives. But the great depravity and corruption of the times in which he lived, and of thofe, whofe annals and Hiftory he writes, may plead an excufe for his, perhaps too refined, fufpicion concerning the interefted motives of human conduct: and his mafterly obfervations, his wife maxims, and that concife energy, with which he draws the characters of men, and defcribes the manners and cuftoms of nations, have placed him in the Temple of Immortality, and will make him for ever be regarded as one of the ableft and moft inftructive of all writers.

I HAVE mentioned thefe three, becaufe they are the flower of the Roman Hiftorians, and have been the admiration of almoft all the great men, who have been eminent in civil life fince their times. If you enquire into the characters of thofe who have made the moft fhining figure in the Britifh fenate, you will find that moft of them were able
mafters

masters of classical learning, that they were well acquainted with these Historians in particular, and that from them they have drawn many examples and maxims, which they have with great propriety applied to the circumstances of their own country.

It is the observation of a polite writer *, that it is unpardonable even in the ladies not to be acquainted with the Greek and Roman Histories. Whether a great many ladies of fashion are utterly unacquainted with them, and think it no reproach to be so, I shall not say; but for a young gentleman, who has had a liberal education, and can have recourse to the original authors, to be ignorant in these articles, would imply a most reproachful negligence and want of inclination to improve himself. For though one may acquire a tolerable knowledge of Greek and Roman affairs from modern translations and compilations, yet they, who are able to go to the original fountains, from which the best of these moderns drew their knowledge, will

* Mr. Hume, Mor and Polit. Essays.

find

find what a difference there is between that pure water, which one drinks at the spring-head, and that which, by running a long way through various channels, has become confused and muddy by a mixture of less pure streams. Indeed the study of some modern works will greatly facilitate your knowledge of these Histories, if read along and compared with the original authors. Hook's Roman History, so far as it has gone, and we hope he will carry it down farther, with the writings of some others concerning Roman affairs, do honour to the English language; and there are several French writers, who are extremely valuable. One * genius indeed of that nation has, beyond all others, in the most masterly manner, pointed out the causes of that grandeur and empire, to which the Romans arrived, as well as those which at last occasioned their declension and fall.

AND here I beg leave to observe, that nothing claims your attention more, when you are reading the History of any nation, than

* President Montesquieu.

thofe circumftances by which it became great, rich, and free, and thofe by which it loft its grandeur, riches, and freedom. What has happened in one nation, may happen in another: if the Romans, by bravery, by temperance, by a warm love of their country, of liberty and truth, attained to greatnefs and empire: if, when they became effeminate and luxurious, if, when a regard to private intereft and pleafure prevailed over that of their country and freedom, they fell a prey to the ambition of an enterprizing genius, and at laft became the conqueft of thofe hardy and incorrupt people, whom they defpifed and contemptuoufly named Barbarians, their fate may ferve as a light to warn others from ftriking upon the fame rocks, and ought to infpire every man of influence in any country to ftudy with attention thofe remarkable changes of manners and of governments which are exhibited to us in Hiftory, and to reflect upon their caufes and confequences, that he may be enabled to conduct himfelf in fuch a manner as may beft prevent his own country from arriving at fuch a ftate as

has

has never failed to bring ruin upon others *.

The downfal of that mighty Empire, which the Roman bravery had been so many ages in erecting, as it was effected by those swarms of uncivilized and hardy Barbarians who came from the northern countries, so it overrun Europe with the unpolished and barbarous manners of those people, who, to use the words of a masterly writer †, " under the " several names of Goths, Vandals, Huns, " Bulgars, Francs, Saxons, and many others, " broke in at several times and places upon " the several Provinces of the Roman Em- " pire, like so many tempests, tore in pieces " the whole fabrick of that government, " framed many new ones in its room, chang- " ed the inhabitants, language, customs, laws,

---

* Hoc illud est præcipue in cognitione rerum salubre ac frugiferum omnis te exempli documenta in illustri posita monumento intueri: inde tibi tuæque reipublicæ, quod imitere, capias; inde fœdum inceptu, fœdum exitu, quod vites. *Liv.*

† Sir William Temple.

" the

"the usual names of places, and of men, and even the very face of nature, where they came, and planted new nations and dominions in their room."

THE view of those governments which were established upon the ruin of the Roman Empire; and the History of the people who lived in them, will afford you but small entertainment; and that knowledge which we can acquire about them, uninteresting and insipid as it is, must originally be sought for in the ridiculous and ungracious annals and chronicles of superstitious Monks. So that as the Greek and Roman Histories, as I observed before, claim your attention on a double account, both the grandeur of the subject, and the elegant manner in which they are wrote; one may perhaps have a double excuse for being less attentive to the History of those times, and less careful of being intimately acquainted with the manners and atchievements of such rough and savage people.

AND

And yet, my Lord, one would not choose to be altogether ignorant of the transactions of the dark ages, or to leave so great a blank in our knowledge of human affairs. Every person who would wish to be acquainted with the source and original of our laws and customs, and to form a general idea of our History, must go back to those distant times, as we like to look at old tapestry which recalls to our minds the modes and customs of our forefathers. "Il faut convenir que tout "homme qui sera curieux de remonter a la "source de nos loix, ou de nos usages, et qui "voudra se former une ideé generale de "notre Histoire, aimera a repasser sur ces "tems eloignés, comme on aime a voir d' "anciennes tapisseries, qui nous rappellent "les modes et les coutumes des nos peres," as the accurate and sensible author of the Chronological History of France observes, with respect to the History of his own country, and which is no less true with respect to that of ours.

LETTER III.

'Tis by a knowledge of the governments which were eſtabliſhed, and the cuſtoms which prevailed in Europe during thoſe periods, that we can alone acquire a juſt idea of the various conſtitutions, under which the European nations now live, and the laws and cuſtoms by which they are at preſent governed: for they may be traced up to thoſe times, and however much they have been changed and altered, as choice, accident, climate, or the genius of ſome leading characters gave an opportunity at different times and in different nations, they derive their original from the manners which prevailed in Europe in the barbarous ages. Even that noble ſyſtem of Britiſh liberty, which has been ſo many ages in perfecting, owes its original to ſome of the laws and cuſtoms of thoſe wild and ſavage nations; this beautiful ſyſtem was found in the woods: " ce beau ſyſteme a eté trouvé dans " les bois", to, uſe the words of preſident Monteſquieu, in that chapter of the Spirit of Laws, in which he delineates the Engliſh conſtitution, alluding to ſome of its nobleſt inſtitutions, ftitutions, which are evidently derived from the manners of the antient Germans, who lived not in polifhed cities, but were fcattered about in an uncultivated and woody country.

BESIDES, the Hiftory of the various arts, which, in thofe dark ages, the haughty tyrants of the Roman See, made ufe of to acquire and maintain an unjuft and pernicious fupremacy over all the chriftian world, and to keep mankind bound in the chains of ignorance and fuperftition, though it offers to our view a picture of human affairs, that is gloomy and difagreeable to the laft degree, may be of confiderable ufe, by raifing in our minds a deteftation of fuch a tyrannical fuperftition, which almoft extinguifhed every generous principle of the human heart, and fo reftrained and debafed the genius and underftandings of men, that there remains no monument of thofe ages, which does not give us reafon to conclude that the generality of Europe was then as grofly ftupid and

and barbarous, as the most remote and unpolished parts of it are at this day.

We need hardly indeed wonder that they, who must have been conscious of perverting a god-like and humane religion to the most ungod-like, and most inhuman purposes, *loved darkness rather than light*, and strove hard to prevent those clouds of ignorance and error which overwhelmed the minds of men, from being dispelled. They knew well that, when these should be removed, the craft and wickedness of their schemes would be seen through, and the world no longer kept under subjection to their tyrannic yoke. In fact, this happened; for when several concurring circumstances, but especially the invention of the art of printing, which was found out about the middle of the fifteenth century, made it impossible to keep mankind longer in the dark; the genius of Europe shone forth, arts and sciences began to flourish, the precious remains of antiquity were studied, the spirit of the antients was admired, and imitated;

imitated; superstition could not stand before such opponents; idle legends fell into discredit, the written oracles of heaven were rationally examined; men found out by them what was truly of divine and what of human origin, and religion was, in a great part of Europe, reformed according to the unerring standard of sacred writ.

THE History of Europe, from the time of the reformation, and for above a century before it, becomes peculiarly interesting both on account of the superior knowledge and improvements which have prevailed since that time, and also because the general policy of Europe, and of its particular governments began to change nearly at that period: the authority of sovereigns, and the rights of the bulk of the people gained ground, and were better ascertained: the haughty pride of inferior tyrants submitted to the power of kings, and the people supported and protected by their sovereigns, assumed a spirit which disdained to be oppressed and trampled upon

upon by those to whom formerly they belonged as mere slaves. The face of Europe was changed, and her governments gradually took that form in which they have since appeared; in some of them the improvements were greater, in others less; in some they were more rapid, in others more slow: in some the power, of which the grandees were deprived, fell principally into the hands of the king, as in France; in others, the bulk of the people acquired a considerable share of it, as in England.

To point out the methods by which those alterations were brought about, and to explain how the interest both of kings and people concurred to prompt them to set bounds to the power of those, who, being absolute in their own domains, could be controuled by no law but that of force, and were only obedient to that state to which they owed allegiance, when it was their interest to be so, or when they durst not rebel: to point out how the natural situation of one

coun-

country, tending to enlarge its commerce and enrich the bulk of the people, made the commons acquire a fway, which was not intended by thofe who broke the power of the great Barons; and to fhew how in another the military difpofition of the ftate, and their fituation with refpect to neighbouring powers, retarded the progrefs of trade, and by keeping the people poor, prevented them from becoming fharers of that authority which their kings affumed, would far exceed the bounds of a letter, and has already been often done in a mafterly manner.

PRESIDENT Montefquieu, who has well merited the noble title of legiflator of the world*, hath with his ufual abilities traced out and developped in his Spirit of Laws the caufes of the great changes, which have happened in the governments and circumftances of every nation of the world: no book is

---

* L'efprit des loix eft le code de tous les peuples, et le prefident de Montefquieu eft le legiflateur de l'univers.
Mes Penfées.

more worthy of your study, none contains a greater fund of knowledge proper for a British nobleman. Henaut, in the concluding remarks on his history of France, hath in a few most instructive pages explained the means by which the French Monarchy acquired its present form; and, though he confines himself to the police of his own country, naturally leads us to form proper reflections upon that of others. There are few things wrote with more judgment and concise neatness, or that in such small bounds present us with so many useful ideas, as his Chronological History of France.

THE History of one's own country claims, indeed, a superior regard to that of any other, especially those periods of it, in which its government underwent confiderable alterations; when its civil or religious policy took a different form; when those privileges, which men hold so dear, were acquired; and when superstition and tyranny, which had long made mankind groan under their oppressive yoke,

yoke, gave way to the happy influence of true religion and freedom. By studying how these advantages and privileges were acquired, we can best learn how they may be maintained, and, perhaps (for there never was a perfect human system of any kind) improved and confirmed.

How much religious and civil freedom are worth preserving, and what a glorious influence they have upon human affairs, you will be convinced by comparing what Europe has been since the reformation with what it was before that period; and that the improvements in every kind, which have taken place since that time, are chiefly owing to this cause will appear evident, if you reflect that those improvements have only taken place in countries where men have thrown off the papal yoke, or where there are great numbers of the people who would wish, and have attempted, to do it. "It has been said that "without Descartes, Newton would perhaps "never have been; it might have been said "with greater propriety that without Luther
"and

" and Calvin, Defcartes would perhaps never
" have been *.

" VOLTAIRE has more than once taken no-
" tice, that it was a pity fuch middling ge-
" niufes as Luther and Calvin fhould have
" made fo many profelytes, while Locke
" and Newton have made fo few : but he for-
" gets to obferve that Locke and Newton
" have had no difciples but in thofe countries
" where Luther and Calvin have been fol-
" lowed, and that they are unknown where-
" ever the doctrine of thofe middling geniufes
" has been profcribed.

* On dit que fans Defcartes, Newton n'auroit peut-être pas eté, et je dis que Defcartes n'auroit peutêtre pas eté fans Luther et Calvin.

M. de Voltaire a dit et redit qu'il etoit trifte que d'auffi mediores efprits que Luther et Calvin euffent faits tant de Profelytes, tandis que Locke and Newton en ont fait fi peu. Mais il ne prend pas garde que Locke et Newton n'ont eu des fectateurs que dans les pais ou Luther et Calvin ont eté fuivis, et qu'ils font inconnus par tout ou la doctrine de ces efprits mediocres a etè profcrite. *Mes Penfées*, CXLIV.

THERE

THESE are the words of a smart writer; and undoubtedly that rational inquiry, which the reformation not only permits but approves of, has had, and must have, a wonderful influence in enlarging the genius and understandings of men.

FROM this period men gradually improved in real knowledge, studied nature both physical and moral in a more manly and rational manner; and at different times, by the strength of some superior geniuses, whose minds were now at liberty to follow truth wherever she should lead them, great lights were struck out. The bewildering methods of reasoning taught by the school-men of the dark ages began to fall into disrepute: men could not, however, all at once throw off the yoke of scholastic fopperies. One folly gave way, and then another, till at last a profound genius of this country (Lord Bacon) taught men how they should study nature, and some time after, Sir Isaac Newton unravelled the system of the universe, and explained its laws with a penetration infinitely

finitely beyond what had been done before, or, indeed, could have been conceived before his time; guided by uncommon modesty, as well as judgment and genius, he built his system upon such experimental principles as will stand the test of ages, and not, like the fanciful schemes of other philosophers, give way to more fashionable dreams. At the same time, mechanics were studied and applied to the purposes of civil life: by this means labour was made easier, and men were enabled to make a better use of those materials with which this earth is so plentifully provided for their comfort and pleasure. Navigation was improved, and an intercourse between the different nations of the world rendered more safe and easy. Society was gradually more polished, and the manners of men civilized; the grossness of the preceding ages was cleared away, and that of Lewis XIV. of the revolution, of Sir Isaac Newton, or call it by what other name you please, was so much refined, as to claim the privilege of being ranked among those few which have merited to be called golden
ones

ones better than that which actually was so.

In such enlightened times has your Lordship been born; perhaps the golden age is not yet over; arts and sciences are not, we hope yet ready to take their flight to regions hitherto not so highly favoured by the muses as this island. Let us however beware of treating them with neglect; if they be disdained or undervalued, they will fly to more worthy votaries, accompanied with every thing that is ingenious and valuable, and leave nothing behind them but ignorance and barbarism. Then will Britain be, what it once was, the despised region of fierceness and barbarity, and not the envied seat of liberty and knowledge. The very idea is shocking enough to inspire every one to do all he can to prevent or retard so dismal a change. The higher one's rank is, the more one can do. But here I have done; your Lordship does not stand in need of any arguments to prompt you to do all you can

LETTER III.

can to prevent your country from falling again into such a state of barbarity, as History represents it once to have been overrun with.

I am, &c.

LETTER IV.

On Biography.

My Lord,

THE pleasure your Lordship takes in reading the lives of illustrious men, is a very happy and a very natural one. As you find it an agreeable and entertaining amusement, so nothing can tend more to your improvement and instruction. We become interested in those persons who make a figure in history, and have performed actions worthy of being transmitted down to posterity and of being admired; we have a natural curiosity to be acquainted with the most remarkable circumstances of their lives, and to know what their conduct was in private as well as in public, as men as well as citizens; but this curiosity, the rules of composition

sition permit not an historian, who proposes to write the general History of any country, to gratify. As his subject is the general History of the country, that of individuals can only be brought into it so far as they had an influence upon public affairs, or helped to bring about those events which are the subject of the historic page. The justness of this rule may be illustrated by the analogy it holds with what is observed in the composition of other works.

In painting, the artist pitches upon some particular action to be the subject of his piece, and no circumstances can with propriety be brought into that piece, which are unnecessary to add strength and spirit to the principal subject. A picture representing the choice of Hercules can with propriety admit of no circumstance of that hero's life, but that single one of his being addressed by the goddesses of virtue and pleasure, exhorted by the one to pursue the manly road of temperance and virtue, allured by the other to follow the luxurious paths of indolence and vice: every other

other part of the History of Hercules is foreign to the subject, and if brought into that piece, would break the unity of the design, divert the attention from the main subject, and render the work irregular and absurd.

In a tragedy which should have for its subject, the death of Cato, none of the actions of that great man could with propriety be exhibited upon the stage, but those, which accompanied his death, and which have an effect to render that event more striking.

The rule holds equally well in History; nothing can with propriety be brought into that of any particular nation, but what tends to give us a just idea of the genius, manners, and customs of the people, of their laws and constitution, of their exploits in war and policy in time of peace, or of whatever else is necessary to make us properly acquainted with their History as a nation. The actions of particular men can be related only so far as they had an influence upon the general affairs of their country; and no other part of their lives, however admirable and worthy of being known, falls properly under the notice and obfervation of a writer who propofes to relate the Hiftory of a nation in general.

But your Lordfhip will readily own, that thofe actions of men, which have an influence upon public affairs, are not the only actions worthy of being known, and that the more private circumftances of their lives are often no lefs fo, nay perhaps are more interefting, and offer to our obfervation more frequent occafions of improvement and inftruction: Hence the utility of Biography appears, which, having the Hiftory of an individual for its fubject, with propriety relates every remarkable circumftance of the life of that individual, confiders his private as well as his public conduct; his behaviour among a circle of friends, as well as his appearances in a public affembly; views him at the head of a

fa-

family, as well as at that of an army; follows him from the senate-house to his private study; and in a word, endeavours to find out and exhibit the real character and portrait of the man as well as of the citizen.

The happiness of the world depends no less upon the conduct of men in their private than in their public capacities; indeed they who have many opportunities of being useful and of doing good in the one, have generally no fewer in the other. They who have it in their power to become eminently serviceable to their king and country by unshaken loyalty and patriotism, have commonly at the same time a large sphere in which they may exercise their private virtues, and must become a blessing or a scourge, and contribute to the prosperity and happiness, or to the distress and uneasiness of many of their fellow creatures. That species of history then, which can with propriety enlarge upon the private, benevolent, and amiable qualities of illustrious men; and by drawing an engaging picture of their virtues, incite

others

others to imitate them in their goodnefs, muft certainly have a friendly influence upon human affairs, and be highly ufeful. They indeed muft be infenfible to every virtuous emotion, who have never felt their hearts fired with a love of virtue and an admiration of great and generous actions, when they were reading the hiftory of great and good men wrote by an able Biographer.

To fucceed well in Biography, confiderable talents are required: the writer muft have a genius that is quick, and fenfibly ftruck by fuch circumftances as are characteriftic * of the perfon whofe hiftory he writes, and know

---

* In a performance, which the author modeftly entitles a Catalogue of the Royal and Noble Authors of England, more light is thrown upon fome characters in a few pages, by a judicious choice of a few diftinguifhing circumftances, than had been done before in fome volumes.

" J'aimerois mieux avoir fait l'hiftoire de ―― qui
" n'a pas plus de dix pages, que la belle, l'admirable,
" l'immortelle hiftoire de ―― qui a dix gros volumes."
Mes Penfées, CCXLV.

how to separate these from such as are common to him with a thousand others. He must have that discernment which can look through the deeds of men, and is not apt to be imposed upon by fallacious appearances: he must neither be enthusiastically fond of his Hero, nor too cool in his interest: he must have that impartiality which is so rarely to be found in Biographers, especially those who write the lives of persons who have been cotemporary with themselves, or lived near their own times. If the life of one who lived in a distant period be the subject, much pains and accuracy are required in reading the authors of that age, and in searching those antient monuments which are necessary to give a just idea of the subject, and to throw light upon it.

When I read the life of an illustrious man well wrote, and reflect what trouble it must have given the author to clear away a heap of rubbish that he might present us with an elegant work, I cannot but reckon myself obliged

obliged to one by whose labour I enjoy so instructive and so agreeable a pleasure*.

I BELIEVE it will be found true by most readers, that they have seldom been more pleased, or less tired with any work, than when they were reading the life of a particular person, especially if it was the life of one, whose turn of mind was somewhat similar to their own; and I have often thought that it was a good way to find out one's genius, to observe what sort of lives please us most, which we like best to talk of, and which make the strongest impression upon our minds. They who discover a greater admiration of the rapid and ungovernable bravery of a Charles XII. than of the sedate and consummate conduct of a Marlborough, and take more pleasure in reading the history of such as bear a nearer resemblance to the Swede, than to the English hero, will pro-

* Ad res pulcherrimas, ex tenebris ad lucem erutas alieno labore deducimur. *Senec.*

bably

bably be found in fact more fit to head a desperate attack than to conduct a rational enterprize. They, who find themselves less tired when reading the life of an able and wise chancellor, or of a great and learned prelate, than of a celebrated general or commander, are, 'tis to be presumed, formed by nature to wear the sacred or civil gown with a better grace, than they could wield the general's staff. I believe, I may add, that those who are more charmed with accounts of such persons as lived in elegant retirement, far removed from the hurry of courts and business, than of those who spend their lives amidst the bustle and intrigues of the world, will find themselves improperly placed, when they entirely forsake their more private way of life, and enter deeply into affairs and public management.

THIS then is one way by which we may find out what path our genius points out to us to pursue, what course it warns us not to follow, and makes us feel to be contrary to our natural disposition. Hence it appears

ex-

extremely proper that young gentlemen fhould have the lives of men of various characters put into their hands before they fet out in life, that thus they may have an opportunity of difcovering what beft fuits their own turn of mind; for fuch as affume a character, that nature never gave them, will hardly ever make a figure in life, be happy in themfelves, or ufeful to the world.

But of all accounts of the actions of great men, thofe which were wrote by the actors themfelves are the moft ufeful and agreeable. Partiality natural to one's felf, may indeed fometimes tempt the writer to varnifh over fuch parts of his conduct as might appear difhonourable, or render his fame lefs glorious; but that fpirit which generally appears in them, that warmth with which a remembrance of what they once acted, infpires the writers; and that intimate knowledge, which they muft have of their fubject, compenfate other difadvantages, ftrike the reader with greater force, and make him enter more feelingly into the interefts of one who is

both

both the actor and writer, than the less animated performances of compilators can possibly do.

Your Lordship will easily recall to your memory examples of this both among the antients and moderns. Who could have wrote the actions of Julius Cæsar with a thousandth part of that eloquence and spirit that he himself does in his admired commentaries? or who could have made us follow Xenophon and his ten thousand Greeks, with such eager anxiety and attention, in that masterly retreat which they made though a vast tract of country amidst every disadvantage and difficulty, as he himself has done, in his Anabasis, with no less skill than he conducted the enterprise.

Among the moderns, we meet with many examples of memoirs of the lives of great men written by themselves in the most lively and instructive manner. Need I mention Sully's Memoirs, from which one can certainly form a
juster

juster idea of the great goodness, consummate abilities, and heroic qualities of his master Henry IV. and of his own capacity and integrity, than can be done from any other of the numerous histories of those times. Cardinal de Retz, that great genius, pushed headlong into affairs and intrigues of every kind by the active impetuosity of his disposition, has drawn in his memoirs, one of the strongest portraits of an extraordinary character that the world ever saw. By fairly laying before us both his good and bad qualities, by exposing his own foibles more freely than any one else could have done, as I have seen it somewhere observed, he hath made his faults useful to the world, and pointed out the dangers and vexatious consequences, which attend that headstrong ambition which can throw every thing into confusion, but knows not how to quiet or compose the storm it has raised; qui fçait brouiller, mais pas denouer, as the French sometimes express themselves when speaking of such characters: there are a great many other memoirs in several modern languages, which are extremely amusing, and

make

make us acquainted with the characters of several great men in a way that comes nearest to personal intimacy.

ALLOW me to add as a proof of the agreeable and interesting nature of this species of writing, that the mere Romance-writer finds no better method of narrating his story in a pleasing and entertaining manner, than by making his hero himself relate his own adventures.

AND since I have happened to name romances, I must beg leave to say that this species of artificial Biography, when executed in a masterly manner, does not want its advantages. Freed from a chain of real events, the author is at liberty to choose such as appear to him most proper to convey whatever moral or instruction he pleases. The landscape-painter, who accurately draws a scene which really exists in nature, deserves to be praised for his skill and labour; but certainly he, WHOSE EYE, as one, who had

him-

himself * a most creative fancy, expresses it with his usual energy,

-----In a fine frenzy rolling,
Doth glance from heaven to earth, from earth to heaven;
And, as imagination bodies forth
The forms of things unknown,-----
Turns them to shape,-----

And with a masterly hand represents a scene adorned with striking beauties, which his fancy enabled him properly to assemble, merits applause both on account of the execution and of the genius necessary for producing such a piece. Thus too, a writer who gives us the history of a fictitious person, and fills up his life with great or instructive events, and by the probability of his narration makes us forget we are reading a romance, interests our passions, and strongly moves every affection of the human mind, must have a genius and talents highly worthy of esteem †.

* Shakespear.
† Ille per extensum funem mihi posse videtur,
Ire, meum qui pectus inaniter angit,
Irritat, mulcet, falcis terroribus implet.

I HOPE

On Biography.

I HOPE you do not fuspect me of recommending the common run of thofe filly things which are offered to the public under the name of romances and novels. Vitious and foolifh, they can only pleafe the debauched, the lazy, the ignorant; and are below the contempt of a man of fenfe and virtue. But there have been fome of another ftamp. Since Don Quixote was wrote in Spanifh, and Gill Blas in French, feveral performances of this kind have appeared in foreign languages as well as in our own, from which we may learn a good deal of the manners of the world, and by laughing at the folly of others be taught how to avoid becoming ridiculous ourfelves.

THERE is one account of the life of an illuftrious perfon, not indeed a modern one, which I cannot help mentioning to you here, both becaufe that divine elegance with which it is wrote, made it antiently be faid, that the mufes * fpoke by the mouth of the author,

* Xenophontis voce mufas quafi locutas ferunt. *Cic.*

and because the generality of critics have been of opinion, that it is not a real but an ideal History of the Life of Cyrus; and all agree that, however true the principal facts may be, the author hath added every circumstance which could embellish it, or render it a perfect model of a religious, a wise and heroic prince. No book deserves to be more warmly recommended to a young nobleman than the Cyropædia. The world has few such books to boast of. No history can have a greater influence in forming the heart to truly noble and generous principles, or present the understanding with a more excellent pattern of virtuous and wise conduct. An admirable example, what a useful and charming work may be produced by a writer of true genius, who, not strictly confined to the narration of real facts, gives his imagination scope to invent such as appear fittest to convey useful instruction in the most agreeable manner.

THERE

On BIOGRAPHY.

THERE is one way of becoming acquainted with the characters of great men, that has always been reckoned among the best methods of acquiring a true idea of their real principles, and of those motives which influenced their conduct and were the springs of their actions: reading their familiar letters. When one is writing to a friend, the heart is open, and discloses those opinions and sentiments, which prudence makes it improper that all the world should be acquainted with, or which perhaps less honourable motives make men cautiously conceal.

OF all the advantages and pleasures, that flow from friendship, none is more agreeable, or gives a more pleasing relief to a mind full of anxious cares, than to have one, into whose bosom we may pour all our secrets, and whose fidelity we are entirely assured of, "præparata pectora in quæ tuto secretum omne "descendat, quorum concientiam minus "quam tuam timeas", as Seneca finely expresses it: so great is this pleasure, that when absent from our friends we still endeavour to enjoy it, and communicate to them by writing those thoughts, those sentiments, those ideas, which we cannot have the happiness of doing by personal conversation. Letters that passed between friends must more than any thing have that turn, and breathe that spirit which those who wrote them had in company, and by these transcripts of their hearts, we are, as it were, introduced into their acquaintance, and become familiar with them.

When we read Tully's Epistles, and those of his friends, we cannot help thinking ourselves intimate with those personages; we enter into their ways of thinking, we conceive what their sentiments would have been in certain circumstances, and are enabled to form a juster idea of their principles and the motives of their conduct, than we could possibly be by any other method. Mr. Melmoth has lately given a proof of this, and shewn what light may be thrown upon a character by accurately comparing and examining familiar letters,

letters, in his ingenious remarks on thofe of Cicero: one would wifh indeed that it had turned out as much to the honour of the orator, as it has done to the ingenuity of his elegant tranflator, and that a man of Tully's abilities and real goodnefs of heart had not fullied them by a conduct fo unfteady.

I OBSERVED before, that, by ftudying to become acquainted with the Hiftory of great men, by reading their memoirs, their letters, or accounts of their lives wrote by able Biographers, we fomehow become acquainted with themfelves, and may thus be faid to be introduced into the beft company. Of what confequence this is, muft be readily acknowledged by every one. Not only the difpofitions and hearts of men take a tincture from thofe with whom they are moft intimate and ftrictly connected, but even their heads and underftandings form themfelves fomewhat into a level with thofe of the people they converfe with, and men in fome meafure become weak or able as the perfons are with whom they fpend the greateft part of their time.

How much does one improve in some people's company, how little can we learn in that of others? How many visits may one make without meeting with any thing but dull ceremony or insipid chit-chat about trifling subjects? Dress, equipage, game! from how many people does one return disgusted and out of humour? How dangerous are some societies, how constrained are we obliged to be in them, and how much on our guard? But in that illustrious society of great men, into which Biography introduces us, we can never receive any hurt, and may often reap much benefit; even faults which were prejudicial to their cotemporaries may be of advantage to us, by teaching us how we may best escape errors into which others fell, and not be imposed upon by similar characters, that may happen to exist within the circle of our own acquaintance. None of Plutarch's heroes will lead us into any foolish party, none of their conversations will be dangerous, none of their friendships fatal; an intimacy with them will not be ruinous or expensive: they will always be at home to receive us, us, and in such a manner as will make us leave them with a warmer affection for them, and a higher esteem of their virtues: the more instruction we receive from them, the greater reason will we have to be convinced that we may receive still more. How happy must he be, who hath contracted such friendship, and put himself under the direction of such guardians, who will be able to advise him about the greatest and smallest affairs, from whom he will hear truth without insolence, be commended without flattery, and after whose example he may form himself?

ALLOW me, my Lord, to conclude this letter with transcribing a few lines from an * author, whom I have just now had in my eye, whose noble sentiments, and lively manner of writing, never fail to warm the heart with a love of virtue, and of whose very faults, it hath with great propriety been said, that they are agreeable †.----- " horum nemo non va-
" cabit, nemo non venientem ad se beatio-
" rem, amantioremque sui demittit ---- nocte

* Senec. † Dulcibus abundat vitiis. *Quintil.*

con-

LETTER IV.

"conveniri et interdiu ab omnibus mortali-
"bus poffunt----- horum nemo annos tuos
"conteret, fuos tibi contribuet: nullius ex
"his fermo periculofus erit, nullius amicitia
"capitalis, nullius fumptuofa obfervatio -----
"feres ex his quidquid voles, per illos non
"ftabit quo minus quantum plurimum cœ-
"peris, haurias. Quæ illum felicitas quam
"pulchra feneƈtus manet, qui fe in horum
"clientelam contulit? habebit cum quibus
"de minimis maximifque rebus deliberet,
"quos de fe quotidie confulat, a quibus au-
"diat verum fine contumelia, laudetur fine
"adulatione, ad quorum fe fimilitudinem ef-
"fingat."

I am, &c.

LETTER V.

Of TASTE;

And of some distinguishing Circumstances of LONDON and PARIS.

My Lord,

IT must appear evident to any one, who, without prejudice, examines the figure which this country has made in its most admired periods for learning and politeness, that a depth of judgment, solidity of understanding, and a power of expressing strong passions with remarkable energy, have been far more its distinguishing characteristics, than delicacy or refinement of Taste.

A BACON, a NEWTON, a LOCKE, have an indisputable title to the palm in profound and rational

rational philosophy. Milton and Shakespear have conceived the noblest ideas, seen through every winding of the human heart, drawn the characters of men, and described every object in nature with a force and expression equal to the greatest masters of antiquity, and beyond any of their modern rivals. But with regard to exactness or refinement of Taste, it will hardly be said, that we do not oftener meet in Milton and Shakespear with what appears extravagant and improbable, than in Corneille, Racine or Voltaire. This last, taking notice of that want of decency and regularity, which may with too much justice be reproached to the English stage, confesses the great marks of genius which appear in our tragedies, and which, if those irregularities were removed, would soon make the English excel the Grecian or French Drama [*]. One

---

[*] En Angleterre, la tragedie est veritablement une action; et si les auteurs de ce pays joignoient á l'activité qui anime leurs pieces un stile naturel avec de la decence et de la regularité, ils l'emporteroient bien tot sur les Grecs et sur les François.
Volt. Ess. sur le Poem. Epiq.

must

must indeed have imbibed strong prejudices, who does not perceive and acknowledge that defect in point of chastity and correctness of taste, which is conspicuous in the best and strongest geniuses among the English writers.

WHENCE this arises, and how it happens, that the English are more remarkable for depth of understanding and sublimity of genius, the French for a certain gentility of manner, and accuracy of Taste, may be worth enquiring into; and as we go along, I may perhaps have some opportunities of pointing out to you, how a nobleman may have it in his power to improve the manner and correct the taste of his country.

You are, I am persuaded, far above the low prejudices of those who cannot bear to be told that the French excel in any thing. I just now quoted one of their writers, allowing the English to be preferable in some things; may not we allow his countrymen to be so in others? Truth ought to be the foundation of all our opinions; and as it is
ab-

LETTER V.

absurd, so nothing can discover a more vulgar and narrow disposition of mind, than to refuse to any country whatever merit truly belongs to it.

As the taste of the metropolis must always have the greatest influence upon that of a whole country, the character of a nation with respect to this article, will commonly be found to be what might be expected from the peculiarly favorable or unfavorable circumstances of its capital. 'Tis generally indeed in the chief city of a country, that those works are produced which determine its character for genius and taste. In every metropolis there must be more incitements and opportunities to improve one's genius than in provincial towns; hence they become the centers whither all naturally tend, whose minds prompt them to acquire the friendship of eminent men, to endeavour to become eminent themselves, to improve their talents, or to enlarge their knowledge and cultivate their understandings:
" Alios

Of TASTE.

" Alios liberalium studiorum cupiditas, alios
" spectacula, quosdam traxit amicitia, quos-
" dam industria latam ostendendæ virtuti
" nacta materiam *." By comparing, therefore, the circumstances of the capitals, and
the opportunities of improvement which they
afford, we may form a probable conjecture
concerning the causes of that difference of
Taste which prevails in any two nations.

LONDON and Paris, the capitals of two
rival kingdoms, the two largest cities, and
the principal seats of arts and sciences in Europe, no less famous in modern, than Rome
and Athens were in ancient times, are governed by customs, and distinguished by circumstances more different than those which
took place in the capitals of the Athenian and
Roman Republicks.

LONDON is the greatest trading city in the
world: Paris has no trade but that of its elegant toys, and ingenious manufactures. Paris is the seat of a famous and great univer-

* Senec.

sity,

sity, and of societies for the improvement of the Belles Lettres, and the Arts; there are no such societies established in London, nor is it the seat of an university. Paris is well provided with public libraries, and with collections of pictures, statues, &c. open to the study and inspection of every one: there are few public libraries, &c. in London: London is the metropolis of a free, Paris of an absolute government. These are some of the principal circumstances which distinguish London and Paris. By reflecting a little upon each of them, we may perhaps be enabled to account for the difference of taste in those two cities.

Commerce, which is attended with so many advantages, and which diffuses plenty, independence and happiness among the bulk of a people, is, however, less favourable to certain accomplishments, and less conducive to an elegancy of taste and manners, than to perhaps more solid and general blessings. By turning the attention of men chiefly to gain, and by continually employing them in pursuit of

Of TASTE. 81

of this object, it leaves them lefs time to ftudy the arts, and to admire the productions of genius and tafte.

Nor, confidering it merely with refpect to the influence it may have upon tafte, can it be fuppofed a circumftance favourable to that of the Britifh metropolis, that London is the greateft fea-port in the world. The intercourfe which this muft create between vaft numbers of its inhabitants and fea-faring people, may even be thought to communicate a little of that roughnefs which is more the characteriftic of the common run of failors than politenefs and refinement. Hence, perhaps, by attributing it to a complaifance to the prevailing humour of their audience, we may account for the low fcenes and vulgar wit we meet with in fome of our dramatic writers, and for that odd drollery which diftinguifhes the performances of a neighbouring maritime nation.

Every advantage is attended with fome inconvenience: let the Parifians, who live in a

G   city

city which is no sea-port, which has no trade but that of some elegant manufactures, and is alone supported by a passion for living perpetually in the capital, so universal among the French *noblesse*; boast of the politeness and refined taste of their metropolis: the citizens of London may glory in what is more substantial, and contributes more to the happiness of its inhabitants, a share of wealth and independence, diffused by liberty and commerce among all ranks of men, which prevents the meanest individual from being enslaved by the greatest, and enables vast multitudes to enjoy those bounties of heaven, which in other places are confined to a small number of mankind. But certainly if we consider commerce only so far as it may have an influence upon taste, it can never be thought to be an advantage; nor can it be supposed a very favourable circumstance to that of this country, that a considerable part of the trade of England is transacted in the metropolis. That of France is carried on in her provincial towns, and the inhabitants of Paris chiefly consist of the *noblesse*, and of those, who,

who, living on their fortunes and not being hurried by business, have leizure to improve their taste, and to cultivate the fine arts.

UNIVERSITIES, I believe it will be denied by none, are the principal seats of *Learning* and *Knowledge* in every country. Even in those ages, when university-learning was of the most ridiculous sort, foppish and bewildering as it must be confessed to have been, it was, however, the best the world then had, and the members of universities were more enlightened and less ignorant than their countrymen. Though there is a certain stiffness and pedantry that sometimes attends men of great erudition, and which gives their manners an aukward look to the people of active life; yet still we may, without being thought partial, affirm, that they must in all probability have a more correct taste; and, by being accustomed to study the noblest models, be more readily struck with the irregularities of works that deviate from the rules observed by the best writers, than other persons can be supposed to be, whose way of life has not led them to improve their taste, or to correct it by those rules, which were observed by the best geniuses of all ages, but especially by the antients. We may even suppose that conversation with men of learning must be of advantage to others; that in places where there are great numbers of men of letters, a certain proportion of learning must by them be communicated to the people; and that there must be a greater chance of meeting with persons who have taken some pains to correct and improve their tastes.

'Tis a nice question, whether or not it tends more to the advancement of real science, that universities and seminaries for the education of youth should be placed in great and populous cities, than in remote and distant villages: the practice of the antients seems to countenance the custom of having them situated in the metropolis, and of educating the youth of fashion in such places, and in sight of such scenes as they must be conversant

fant with and deeply interefted in, when they come to perform their different parts in life. Epaminondas, the laft year of his life, faid, heard, faw, did the fame things as at that time of life when he began to be inftructed. " Epaminondas la derniere anné de fa vie, " difoit, ecutoit, voyoit, faifoit les memes " chofes que dans l'age ou il avoit com- " mencé d'etre inftruit." This obfervation made by a very good judge *, when fpeaking of the difference of antient and modern education, and illuftrated by naming one of the greateft characters that ever appeared in the world, as an example of it, muft give a great fanction to the antient manner of education.

But whether upon the whole it may be of advantage, or not, that young gentlemen fhould be educated in great cities, or in places retired and confecrated to the mufes alone, is not neceffary to be determined to prove what I cannot help being perfuaded of, that the univerfity of Paris has had a mighty in-

* Montefquieu.

fluence in correcting and improving the taste of the French metropolis, and in diffusing a sort of critical accuracy among its inhabitants; while at the same time the members of the university, by living in so great a city, and conversing with people of active life, have many opportunities of improving in politeness and a knowledge of the fine arts, which can be met with no where but in the capital of a kingdom.

The university of Paris is a great body, and endued with very ample privileges: it consists of about ten colleges, which enjoy the full rights of the university, and I believe, about thirty others, whose rights and privileges are not so great. It can hardly be supposed that such foundations, consecrated to the arts and sciences, will have no influence in communicating a taste for the muses to a city, whose inhabitants must have so much intercourse with learned men. Let us suppose the colleges which are now placed at Oxford or Cambridge to have been erected in different parts of London, can it be be imagined that this would not have had a great influence in communicating knowledge and taste to the whole city, or that the conversation of so many men of learning and genius would not have had a good effect?

But besides the university, there are several societies established in Paris expresly for the improvement of taste. The French academy for the improvement of eloquence and poetry: The royal academy of Inscriptions and Belles Lettres, established in 1663, for cultivating the Belles Lettres, explaining antient monuments, and transmitting to posterity the remarkable events of the Monarchy by medals, &c. The royal academy of Painting * and Sculpture, under the government of a director, who is appointed by the

---

* It is with the greatest pleasure we observe the good effects of the Society for the encouragement of arts, manufactures and commerce. A society which, without neglecting what tends more immediately to the improvement of agriculture, and the necessary arts of life, gives the most honourable encouragement to those that are elegant

the king, a chancellor, four rectors, one of whom attends every quarter, and twelve professors, who attend each of them a month by turns, direct the studies of the pupils, propose models to them, and correct their designs.

There is also a royal academy for the improvement of architecture, in which instructions

elegant and ornamental. Had such a society been instituted thirty years ago, London would, by this time, have been the grand seat of arts, as it is the envied seat of freedom. From the exhibitions that have already been made, we may conceive what twenty years gradual improvement will produce. Some of the drawings—prints—landscapes— and even History-pieces, exposed to public view, discovered both genius and execution. The premiums must excite emulation, which is all that Englishmen want to enable them to shine in any art. The experience of a few years will demonstrate, that genius is not wanting, that liberty is favourable to Taste, and that it was owing to some accidental circumstances that the English have not excelled as much in the fine arts, as in profound science. What may we not expect under the auspicious reign of a Prince, who has
him-

ſtructions are given gratis, and prizes annually diſtributed to incite the emulation of the ſtudents.

AMONG the different circumſtances which diſtinguiſh London and Paris, none is more remarkable than this, that the latter is well ſupplied with great public libraries, with large collections of pictures, ſtatues, prints, and every curioſity of nature or art*, open to the inſpection

himſelf a diſtinguiſhed taſte for the fine arts, and has aſcended the throne at a time when the genius of his ſubjects is turned that way, and only ſtands in need of royal and generous protection to convince the world, that in a free country every art may be brought to perfection. 'Tis with the greateſt pleaſure we perceive that it depends upon ourſelves to make every thing here as favourable to the fine arts as in Paris, and then the effects of liberty will appear conſpicuous. When this letter was wrote, though the Society for Arts was ſet on foot, it was not much known, and no proofs of its happy influence had been given, which is now with the utmoſt joy ſeen and acknowledged.

* Every circumſtance now becomes favourable, and every thing that was wanting to make London as poliſhed and elegant as it is rich and great, will gradually be

inspection of every one; and which, by being so common and of such *easy access*, cannot fail of sometimes giving young people an opportunity of discovering that they have a genius, which in other countries, where the generality of the world seldom have an opportunity of viewing the noble productions of art, those who are endued with equal capacities never have it in their power to discover or perhaps even to *feel*. You may easily conceive that there are many in this great city of London, who, if they had an opportunity of viewing collections of the works of the great masters, would *feel* that nature had given them talents to relish the fine arts, and perhaps to become celebrated artists themselves, who at present, having no

be supplied. The British Museum exceeds any thing of the kind in Paris, and is worthy so large and opulent a city as London. Magnificent at present, it must be still encreasing by the donations of the curious and learned. Its plan is extensive, its regulations good. The studious may read, and philosophers examine the productions of nature: there is something to suit every one, and all have as easy access to this public collection, as is consistent with order and propriety.

such

Of TASTE.

such opportunity, pass obscurely through life, without bringing to light those talents with which they were endued, and which, if properly cultivated, might have been an ornament to the world.

Any one who has been at Paris' may remember what fine collections of pictures are open to the public inspection, and what numbers of young people he must often have met with at the Luxembourg palace, viewing its famous gallery, as well as the noble collections of the works of great masters, which are to be seen in its other apartments. The Duke of Orleans's collection at the *Palais-Royal*, one of the best on this side the Alps, is not sullenly shut up from public view, or open only to those who give high bribes to his servants; but at particular hours any one, who has a taste for enjoying the beauties of the painter's art, may have an opportunity of viewing capital pieces of the most famous hands of the different schools, and of such as are of the most opposite styles. And for those who have a curiosity to form an idea of pictures,

LETTER V.

pictures, statues, edifices, gardens, and of whatever else the ingenious art of engraving can give us a notion, there is a public collection of prints and drawings, so ample as can hardly fail to gratify the wishes of the most curious and inquisitive. Besides these public collections, the private houses of a great many noblemen contain something worth seeing, and any one can have easy access to most of them.

Of what advantage this must be, you will readily conceive, and how much it must tend not only to give true geniuses an opportunity of discovering their talents, but to improve the taste of those who have no extraordinary capacity: by being accustomed frequently to look at what is excellent, one becomes in some degree a judge, and is apt to be disgusted at the sight of what is unnatural and bad; as by often hearing good music, even those, who have no remarkable taste that way, acquire a delicacy of ear, which is shocked with what is discordant and unharmonious.

Of TASTE.

BESIDES, one can seldom fail to meet at those places with some people; who, being themselves sensibly struck with beauties or faults, are prompted by their strong natural feelings to make pertinent observations, and thus help to form the judgments of others to a right taste, and are themselves improved by the conversation and remarks of those around them.

NOTHING surprizes foreigners who come to London more than the scarcity of such public collections in so great a city, and the difficulty and expence of procuring a sight of what is in the private houses of the great! What vast sums are expended in buying pictures and statues, and how are they afterwards buried and made useless for the improvement of taste! Perhaps were these more exposed to public view, it might help in some measure to correct the taste, and prevent the great and opulent of this nation from being so often imposed upon, in these articles.

A NOBLEMAN of the higheſt rank hath indeed lately ſet a generous example, by opening a room containing a collection of models of the antique ſtatues, and by permitting any one to enjoy the pleaſure of viewing models of theſe precious remains of antient art, and artiſts to copy from them : it were to be wiſhed that this example was followed; the lovers of the fine arts would then have reaſon not only to admire what the Duke of Richmond himſelf has done, but to be grateful to him for leading the way, and giving a truly noble example to others of treating the arts and artiſts in a generous manner.

SUCH indulgence would ſoon make Britain not only the ſeat of profound philoſophy and ſolid knowledge, but of taſte and refinement in the elegant arts. In vain, will the climate be objected to this wiſhed-for pre-eminence; London and Antwerp are ſituated in the ſame degree of north latitude. But where were Rubens and Vandyke born? and though, perhaps, it ſhould be allowed that the climate is

not

Of TASTE.

not so favourable as that of some other places, the capital of Great Britain has one advantage which may well be supposed to compensate smaller ones, which attend other cities, particularly the metropolis of the French Monarchy: London is the capital of a free, Paris of an absolute government. But the consideration of the influence this naturally has upon taste, would open too large a field to enter upon at the conclusion of a letter. I must therefore delay it, till I do myself the honour of writing to you again.

I am, &c.

LETTER VI.

On the INFLUENCE of LIBERTY upon TASTE, and of the Age of AUGUSTUS.

MY LORD,

IN a letter which I lately did myself the honour to write to your Lordship, I took notice of some circumstances which distinguish Paris from London, and which, considered only so far as they have an influence upon the *Belles Lettres* and Taste, seem favourable to the metropolis of France. I shall in this, as I promised, endeavour to shew what influence the different degrees of freedom enjoyed by the two countries, of which London and Paris are the capitals, may naturally be imagined to have upon these articles.

I DONT

I don't know how it hath become a pretty common opinion that the strongest efforts of genius will probably be made by those, who enjoy Liberty, and are inspired by its animating influence; but that justness and refinement of Taste will generally be found to be more improved among the subjects of an absolute, than among those of a free government.

That the first of these propositions is true, I shall readily own; the History of all ages, the noble monuments of all free countries, confirm the truth, that Liberty appears attended with whatever is great, spirited, or ingenious: that the second is false, I am persuaded, may be proved from History too, as well as from the nature of the thing; and the same monuments bear witness that freedom has also in her train, genuine elegance, severe justness of taste, natural, simple, and unaffected truth.

Mr. Pope himself, who was as remarkable for his judgment as poetical genius, seems inadvertently to have given countenance to the opinion, that an absolute government is more favourable to the improvement of Taste, than a free one, in those lines of his Essay on Criticism, where he touches upon the progression of the fine arts when they were banished from Italy.

But soon by impious arms from Latium chas'd
Their antient bounds, the banish'd muses pass'd;
Thence arts o'er all the northern world ad-
    vance,
But critic learning flourish'd most in France:
The rules a nation, born to serve, obeys,
And Boileau still in right of Horace sways.

Mr. Pope's authority justly claims the highest respect; but whatever regard is due to so great a name, let it never carry us so far as to believe that those who are *born to serve,* naturally *obey rules* in the fine arts and Belles Lettres (for of these he is talking) better than those who are born free.

This opinion that refinement and elegance will probably be more studied and improved among the subjects of an absolute, than among those of a free government, seems to have taken rise from a partial observation of the state of Taste in the French Monarchy in modern times, and of what happened in Rome, when Octavius made himself master of her liberties and of the world.

But, notwithstanding that polite figure which the ages of Augustus and Lewis XIV. will for ever make in the annals of the world, I am persuaded it may be laid down as a certain maxim, that in every country, not only genius, but Taste also, will be found to be in proportion to freedom, unless the influence of this general law be counteracted by inferior circumstances and accidents, as any general law, either in the physical or moral world, may be observed to be in many particular instances.

To deny the truth of this assertion, one must forget in what countries the best models

dels of natural and elegant compositions of all kinds were produced; at what time genuine Taste began to be cultivated in those countries, when it was carried to its utmost perfection, and when it began to decline and give way to what was unnatural and false.

WHEN did the inhabitants of any, even the most civilized absolute monarchy that ever existed under heaven, discover so refined, so elegant; so correct a Taste, as the citizens of the free states of Greece did? Did ever any one who was born the subject of an absolute prince more strictly *obey* and severely follow those *rules* which good sense and nature pointed out to be just, than they did, who in those states were *born free?* It cannot be said with any justice that they did: nor did ever any one appear, who was born after the Roman emperors had established their power upon the ruins of Liberty, that could dispute for the prize of elegant and just composition with those who were born and educated in better days.

As

As the age of Auguſtus is prior in time to that of Lewis XIV. I ſhall firſt endeavour to obviate the argument againſt the friendly influence, that Liberty undoubtedly has upon Taſte, which may be brought from the elegance and exquiſite beauty of the works of the Auguſtan age; and to ſhew that we are indebted, for the noble compoſitions of that age, not to the influence of Auguſtus's Supreme Power, but to the influence of that Liberty, which, unfortunately for the world and true Taſte, he overthrew, and which had already made Rome the ſeat of genius and refinement, before fortune had raiſed Octavius to imperial ſway, or he had aſſumed to himſelf thoſe powers, which formerly were divided among the different ranks of the Roman people.

Liberty indeed cannot alone, or all at once, refine the genius or Taſte of mankind: other circumſtances muſt concur, but Liberty is ſtill the animating cauſe, and a *total* deprivation of it would ſoon be found to extinguiſh every ſpark both of genius and Taſte.

LETTER VI.

A people *may* be free, and yet rough and unpolished in their Taste as well as manners; but a nation of *slaves must* either discover no Taste at all, or a vitiated and false one. The Romans long retained a certain roughness of manner, and despised elegance and refinement. Their first attempts in composition, like those of every other nation, that begins to extend its dominion and consequence in the world, and to form its government and laws, were rude and barbarous, and their first productions in the fine arts rough and unpolished. But when their constitution was fully established, when their Taste in eloquence began to be refined, when Carthage and the world bowed before the Roman Eagle, when the governors of conquered provinces brought immense wealth to Rome, and raised families whose great opulence enabled them to cultivate and encourage every thing that was elegant and fine, and when the muses had forsaken Greece, no longer now the seat of Liberty; then did the Romans, under the direction of the learned who came from that country, begin to study the elegancies of Taste,

Taste, to love the arts, and to polish the roughness of their style and manner.

It will in vain be objected against the happy influence of Liberty, that the Romans, or any other free people, were for a long time rough and unpolished. A multiplicity of causes may retard improvements in elegance and the fine arts. The Lacedemonians were free as well as the Athenians; but as among the first every refinement was discouraged, and among the latter every thing ingenious and polite was held in the highest esteem, their characters for learning and politeness are extremely different. The rusticity of the antient Romans proves nothing. But if we consider how short a period intervened from their beginning to study the arts, till they lost their freedom; and reflect that the despotism of their emperors put a sudden and unnatural stop to further improvement, it will afford a convincing proof, that liberty is favourable and arbitrary power unfavourable to the liberal arts. That this was the case will appear evident from the best authorities.

LETTER VI.

THERE is a remarkable passage in Tully (De claris oratoribus) in which speaking of M. Cato, after having highly commended his great and various talents as an orator, he owns that his style was antiquated, and that he made use of some barbarous words, for so, says he, they then spake *; and confessing that he was not sufficiently polished, he adds, as a reason or excuse for it, that with respect to the age in which they lived, Cato was so old that there remained no writing of any one who was more antient, that was worth reading †. Yet M. Cato, as we are expressly told in the same Dialogue, died only eighty three years before Cicero was consul ‡.

---

* Antiquior est ejus sermo, et quædam horridiora verba, ita enim tum loquebantur.

† Nec vero ignoro, nondum esse satis politum hunc oratorem . . . . quippe cum ita sit, ad nostrorum temporum rationem vetus ut nullius scriptum extet dignum quidem lectione, quod sit antiquius.

‡ Qui mortuus est annis LXXXIII. ipsis ante me consulem.

THUS

Thus it appears evident from the opinion of the beft judges, the moft eloquent of the Romans themfelves, that the Roman ftyle and manner remained long rough and unpolifhed. Active and warlike, living perpetually amidft the din of arms, or interefted and bufied in forming their government and fixing their laws, they had no time to apply to what was elegant and refined; " nec enim " in conftituentibus rempublicam, nec in " bella gerentibus nafci cupiditas dicendi fo- " let*. 'Twas after their republic had acquired its juft form, and the enemies, which furrounded them on every hand, were fubdued, and no longer in a condition to keep them in a perpetual alarm, and after the haughtieft of their rivals were humbled, that the Romans, now bleft with fome fhare of quiet and fecurity, began to ftudy what was refined, and not only to be careful to fay what was true and juft, but to fpeak and write in an elegant manner.

* Cic. de Clar. Orat.

LETTER VI.

BEFORE this time, indeed, while they were busied in forming their constitution, and reducing each state in Italy, one after another, to a dependency upon that of Rome, we must suppose that a certain sort of oratory, such as their language, yet unpolished, could afford, and capable of affecting a rough and brave people, flourished among them. We know that this was actually the case, and that many of the citizens acquired great authority by speaking; but it was not by an eloquence that would have charmed them in their politer days, but by a plain sort of rhetoric, like that of L. Cassius, who had great influence, not by his eloquence, but yet by what he said, " Multum potuit, non eloquentia, sed dicendo tamen," as Tully observes *, for the people knew he was a man of severe virtue, and on this account he had great credit with them †. 'Twas the character of the man, and what he said, not the manner

---

* Cic. de Clar. Orat. † Severitate popularis. Ibid.

in which he said it, that had an influence upon the martial and honest spirits of the Romans in those days of incorrupted integrity.

But though we find that it was late before the Romans began to study the elegancies of style and composition, when they actually applied the force of their genius to acquire these accomplishments, the high Roman spirit, nursed by freedom, and made manly and bold by that independence, and share of consequence in the state, which every citizen of Rome possessed, enabled them to make as rapid a progress in oratory and the fine arts, as they had formerly done in conquering the world. In the same dialogue, in which the great master of Roman eloquence informs us, that no writings of any one before the age of the elder Cato were worth reading, he gives it as his opinion that the Latin tongue had arrived to full maturity, and Roman eloquence attained its almost utmost perfection, in the person of L. Crassus, who, in an oration much admired by all good judges,

judges, which he made in the 34th year of his age, the very year that Tully was born, gave eminent proofs of his confummate abilities, as an accomplifhed orator *.

Thus we fee that for about a century before the birth of Cicero, while Rome was yet free, eloquence was continually making rapid progrefs to perfection, 'till at laft confummated in the perfon of this great man, the fame tyrannic ftroke, that fevered Tully's head from his body, gave a fatal and finifhing blow to the Roman liberty and eloquence; and, as Seneca fays of Cato and freedom, eloquence and liberty, which it was impoffible to feparate from each other, perifhed and were extinguifhed together, " fimulque extincta funt, quæ nefas erat di-" vidi;" for from that moment, oratory had

* Hæc Craffi cum edita oratio eft, quam te fæpe legiffe certo fcio, quatuor & triginta tum habebat annos, totidemque annis mihi ætate præftabat. His enim coff. eam legem fuafit, quibus nati fumus: quod idcirco pofui, ut, dicendi latinè prima maturitas in qua ætate extitiffet, poffet notari, et ut intelligeretur jam ad fummum pœne effe perductam.

fallen

fallen from its perfection, and gradually became more and more falfe, unnatural, and widely different from the chafte model of the true and genuine eloquence of the days of freedom.

THAT the Roman eloquence muft have had a mighty influence in improving a good Tafte in every thing elfe can hardly be queftioned. The ftudy of this art has by the beft judges been allowed to be naturally connected with whatever is graceful and elegant, or can tend to improve or embellifh the powers of the human mind. In every country where eloquence is a neceffary accomplifhment for thofe who expect to make a figure in the ftate, or to be eminent among their fellow citizens, it may reafonably be fuppofed, that as the tafte in oratory improves, the general Tafte of the nation muft at the fame time be corrected, and its genius prepared for producing noble and juft works of every kind, whenever the attention of the people fhall be turned to the ftudy of the fine arts.

BUT,

BUT, besides the natural tendency of that perfection in oratory to which the Romans had attained in the days of freedom, there were several other circumstances that contributed to refine the Taste of Rome, and to form those immortal writers who flourished in the last age of the republic.

THE conquest of Greece discovered to the Romans, scenes very different from any they had yet seen in the various countries they had formerly subdued. By creating an intercourse, and making them acquainted with the most ingenious and elegant people that ever existed upon earth, it must have had a mighty influence to form their genius, and to give them a taste for what was polite and refined. That this was actually the case you will find to have been the opinion of the best judges among the Romans themselves, and you will meet with various proofs of it in almost all their classic writers. " Multas (artes) ad animorum cor-
" porumque cultum nobis eruditissima omni-
" um gens invexit," to use the words of the
great

great Roman Hiſtorian *. 'Twas the Greeks who taught the Romans almoſt every genteel and graceful exerciſe, and every liberal and elegant accompliſhment.

Before the time of the firſt Macedonian war, the Romans had little intercourſe with the Greeks. Their ambaſſadors had indeed, about twenty years before that period, appeared for the firſt time in the principal cities of Greece, and they had entered into a league againſt Philip, as auxiliaries to the Ætolians † in a war which was carried on againſt that king during more than ten years immediately preceding the firſt Macedonian war.

But from the time that this latter war was concluded, that is, from about ninety years before the birth of Cicero, and about four after the end of the ſecond punic war, the Romans had more and more intercourſe with the Greeks, travelled into their country, and ſtudied Arts and Sciences under Grecian maſters. The conſequences of this war gave

* Liv. Lib. 39. † Liv. Lib. 26. cap. 24.

occaſion

occasion to several embassies to Rome from Macedon, and from several of the states and cities of Greece; and the behaviour of the Roman general, after he had conquered Philip, seems to have been the most proper imaginable to conciliate the minds of the Greeks to make them conceive a favourable opinion of the Romans, and wish to cultivate a friendly correspondence with them. He insisted with the senate, and at last obtained his request, that freedom should be restored to all the cities of Greece, and at the Isthmian games, when vast multitudes were gathered together from all parts, and with the most anxious expectation waited to hear what was to become of Greece, and what their fortune was to be, the Roman general, in his own name, and in that of the Senate, ordered freedom, and a liberty of living according to their own laws and institutions to be proclaimed to all the states of Greece that had been subjected to the dominion of the kings of Macedon: " liberos, immunes, " suis legibus esse jubet Corinthios," &c. But your Lordship will read the whole passage

with

On the INFLUENCE of LIBERTY, &c. 113

with a great deal of pleasure, as it is most charmingly related by Livy in his thirty third Book: You will there see, with what rapture the Greeks heard the dear names of liberty and freedom proclaimed, with what grateful embraces they had almost stifled the Roman Consul, what eulogiums they bestowed upon the Romans; and from thence be easily led to conceive what a favourable opportunity this must have been for beginning a mutual intercourse and correspondence.

The inhabitants of Italy, who went to Greece upon this expedition, must have acquired some knowledge of the Greek language as well as of the Grecian manners and customs; and a great number of Roman captives, who had been taken during the war with Hannibal and sold as slaves, and who had now lived several years in different parts of Greece*, being restored to liberty, and returning to Rome with Flaminius, we may imagine would diffuse among their country-

* Liv. lib. 34. cap. 50.

men a knowledge of the Greek language, and a taste for the refinements of Greece hitherto unknown in Italy; besides, a great many captives and hostages of high rank adorned his triumph *, and during their residence at Rome could not fail to have much influence in inspiring the Romans with a relish for the politeness of their country.

Not long after this, when the unhappy Perseus was defeated by Paulus Æmilius, the inhabitants of Rome had still greater opportunities of improving by conversation with Greeks; for when Æmilius returned in triumph, a great many ingenious men came with him to Rome. These, in all probability, were the best men of Greece, who being represented by vile informers and betrayers of their country as enemies to the Roman interest, were called upon to appear at Rome, and answer for their conduct †. Pausanias,

* Ante currum multi nobiles captivi obsidesque, inter quos Demetrius regis Philippi filius fuit, & Armenes, Nabidis tyranni filius, Lacedæmonius. Liv. lib. 37.

† Liv. lib. 45. cap. 31.

in his account of Achaia, makes their number to have been more than a thousand; and among these were the famous Historian Polybius and his father Lycortas, prætor of the Achæans, a son and father worthy of each other, and of the friendship of Philopæmen. Such men, we may naturally suppose, must have had a great influence to inspire the Romans with a love of Greek letters, and to improve their taste; and we know that this was the case; for to the instructions of a Polybius did the Romans owe one of the greatest and most accomplished men their country ever produced *.

The Romans themselves too must have returned to Rome, after the defeat of Perseus, with a high admiration of Greece, and great-

* Omnibus belli et togæ dotibus, ingeniique et studiorum eminentissimus sui sæculi.

Scipio tam elegans liberalium studiorum omnisque doctrinæ et auctor et admirator fuit, ut Polybium, Panætiumque, præcellentes ingenio viros domi militiæque secum bahuerit. Vell. Paterc. Lib. 1.

ly improved in their taste by a view of the elegant productions of that country. Æmilius, accompanied with his son Scipio, then a youth in his seventeenth year, had found leisure after his victorious campaign to make a tour through Greece*, and to take a view of the beautiful monuments of antient art with which it abounded. In this tour, as Plutarch informs us, " He eased the people's " grievances, reformed their government, " and bestowed gifts upon them;" which could not fail to make him and his attendants as agreeable to the Greeks, as a view of the exquisite beauties of their country seems to have been to him. Both Plutarch and Livy take notice of the rapture with which Æmilius himself beheld the fine works of the Grecian artists: the former tells us, that when in Olympia he viewed the statue of Jove, he uttered these celebrated words, " This " Jupiter of Phidias is the very Jupiter of " Homer," and Livy, in his manner, thus strongly expresses it ----- " Jovem velut præ- " sentem intuens, motus animo est," both

* Liv. lib. 45. cap. 27.

which

which accounts may convince us with what extreme fenfibility Æmilius perceived the beauties of the imitative arts, and with what an improved tafte and relifh for them, he and his attendants muft have returned to Rome. For though the behaviour of Æmilius himfelf only is mentioned, we may eafily imagine that many of his train were ftruck with the fame beauties, and carried with them to Rome, and propagated among their fellow-citizens, a high opinion of the noble and elegant genius of the Greeks. Æmilius indeed, as Livy fays, made this tour with no great croud of attendants*, but we may naturally fuppofe that they were the moft ingenious and learned of his army, and the moft capable of making ufeful obfervations for the improvement of their own country.

About ten years after the triumph of Æmilius, the Athenians fent Carneades and fome other philofophers ambaffadors to Rome. Upon their arrival the moft ftudious and

---

* Profectus cum haud magno comitatu. Lib. 45.

ingenious of the Roman youth waited upon them, heard them with inexpressible pleasure, and were charmed with the eloquence of Carneades in particular *. We may from this infer, that the Greek language was pretty commonly understood among the most ingenious of the Romans even at that time, 'else how could they be so charmed with the Orations of Carneades who spoke in Greek? But from this period the genius of the Romans seems to have been so much turned to the study of the Greek language, philosophy, and eloquence, that they were considered as essential parts of a liberal education among them, and almost every man of fashion at Rome could speak and write in Greek. This taste seems to have made such rapid progress, that even the rigid Cato, who had alarmed the Roman Senate about the dangerous influence of Carneades, and the bad effects which might arise from the study of the Greek language and philosophy †, could not himself resist the charm, but in his old age applied to the

* Plut. in Cat.
† Plut. in Vit. Cat.

study

study of that tongue *. From this time it became more and more uncommon to meet with any one in Rome, but of the lowest rank, who was not pretty well acquainted with Greek.

During the Mithridatic war, a great number of the principal and most polite of the Athenians came to Rome, driven from home by the miseries of their own country. Conversation with such people must have afforded the Romans the best opportunities of improvement. This we find was actually the case: Tully wholly applied himself to cultivate his taste and manner under such masters †; and as Cicero himself certainly owed

---

* Cic. Acad. Quæst. Lib. 2.

† Eodem tempore cùm princeps academiæ Philo cum Athenienfium optimatibus, Mithridatico bello, domo profugiffet Romamque veniffet totum me ei tradidi.

Commentabar declamitans (fic enim nunc loquuntur) fæpe cum M. Pifone, et cum Q. Pompeio, aut cum aliquo quotidie; idque faciebam multum etiam Latinè, fed Græcè fæpius; vel quod Græca oratio plura ornamenta

owed a great deal to the inſtructions he got from them, ſo we may reaſonably conclude that the fine writers of the Ciceronian age were greatly improved by converſation with Greeks, reading Greek authors, and viewing the exquiſite productions of Grecian art.

As in the laſt century of their republic, the Romans became acquainted with the ingenious men of Greece, ſo at different times of the ſame period the works of the fine writers who had flouriſhed in that country in its free and beſt days, and the elegant and inimitable productions of Grecian art were brought to Rome, and became models for the Romans to ſtudy and improve by.

BEFORE the famous ſiege of Syracuſe, which happened during the time of the ſecond punic war, " Rome had never ſeen or known

namenta ſuppeditans, conſuetudinem ſimiliter Latinè dicendi afferebat, vel quod a Græcis ſummis doctoribus, niſi Græcè dicerem, neque corrigi poſſem neque doceri.
Cic. de Clar. Orat.
" any

" any superfluous curiosities, nor were any
" rarities or exquisite pieces of art that shew-
" ed an elegant and polite taste to be found
" there;" but after this city was taken,
Marcellus, by carrying to Rome the fine
statues and paintings with which Syracuse
abounded, " first taught the Romans to ad-
" mire and value the Grecian arts, and gave
" them a taste and relish for those exquisite
" performances which never had been under-
" stood before *.

WHEN Flaminius triumphed over Philip,
he brought to Rome several elegant pieces of
sculpture in marble, and brass, and a great
many vases carved with exquisite art. Most
of these he had taken from the king, and
some of them from the states and cities through
which he passed, but all of them, 'tis probable, were the workmanship of Greek artists †.

* Plut. in Vit. Marcel.
† Signa ærea et marmorea transtulit, plura Philippo
adempta, quam quæ ex civitatibus cœperat.
—— Vasa multa omnis generis, cælata pleraque,
quædam eximiæ artis.   Liv. Lib. 34.

LETTER VI.

WHAT an immense collection of pictures and statues adorned the famous triumph of P. Æmilius, is well known: they were drawn upon seven hundred and fifty carriages, and a whole day was hardly sufficient to give the Romans time to behold this splendid show. At the same time, a vast number of vessels, valuable as well for their largeness as the beauty and strong *relievo* of their engraved work, were brought to Rome*; and the first library in that city consisted of books, which Æmilius permitted his son to take from Perseus †. Many of the inhabitants of Rome must have had an opportunity of improving by reading these books. The first intimacy between Scipio and Polybius, as this Historian himself informs us, took its rise from a mutual intercourse, occasioned by his borrowing some of them from Scipio, who politely lent them to him, and took great pleasure in conversing with so sensible a man concerning the subjects of which they treated.

* Plut. in Vit. Æmil.
† Id. et ibid.

ABOUT twenty years after this, when the Conful Mummius took Corinth, with what an additional number of noble pieces of Grecian art Rome was adorned from the spoils of that elegant city, every one knows; and the famous rusticity and want of taste of Mummius, who, when he was about to transport the pictures and statues of the greatest masters to Italy, told those who were to carry them, that if any of them were lost, they should find new ones in their place, will for ever be remembered, and perhaps afford a suspicion, that at that time there were still some remains of rusticity among the Romans, else how can we suppose that any man of so high a rank could be so extremely ignorant and unpolished?*

WHAT I have hitherto mentioned, happened before the birth of Cicero. I shall only

---

* Mummius tam rudis fuit, ut, capta Corintho, cum maximorum artificum perfectas manibus tabulas, ac statuas in Italiam portandas locaret, juberet prædici conducentibus, si eas perdidissent, *novas eos reddituros.*

Vell. Paterc.

take notice of one addition to the literary treasure of Italy, which was made about twenty years after Tully was born, the Library of Appellicon, that Sylla brought from Athens, and which contained a fine collection of books, particularly the original works of Ariſtotle and Theophraſtus*, authors the fitteſt of any to promote a genuine and elegant taſte, the greateſt and beſt critics, and among the beſt writers which Greece had produced. The works of Ariſtotle have ever been, and will continue to be, the great ſtandard of juſt criticiſm in compoſitions of every kind†.

Thus I have given you a ſhort ſketch of the growing intercourſe which the Romans had with the inhabitants of Greece, of the

---

* Plut. in Vit. Syl.

† Peripatetici autem etiam hæc ipſa, quæ propria oratorum putas eſſe adjumenta, atque ornamenta dicendi ab ſe peti vincerent oportere: ac non ſolum meliora, ſed etiam multa plura Ariſtotelem Theophraſtumque de his rebus, quam omnes dicendi magiſtros, ſcripſiſſe.   Cic. de Orat. Lib. 1.

progress their language made at Rome, and of the importation of the works of Greek writers and ingenious artists with which Italy was enriched at different times, from the conclusion of the first Macedonian war, till some time after the birth of Cicero. That these circumstances must have been favourable for promoting a genuine taste among the Romans, will hardly be denied.

HORACE observes with a seeming regret, that it was late before his countrymen applied the force of their genius to the study of the fine writings of Greece; but perhaps they began to attend to, and relish those noble models at a time the most proper to enable them to excel, or produce works capable of rivaling their charming exemplars. Had they done it sooner, their language, yet unformed, had been incapable of producing what was excellent, and their manners and genius, too rough and unpolished, had been less happily prepared for relishing the beauties of the elegant compositions of Greece, and for cultivating the fine

fine arts. We know 'tis no favorable circumstance to the improvement of an individual, that one begins too early to study any art or science. Incapable of making any progress at a premature period of life, the mind retains a disgust and unwillingness to renew the attempt at a more proper season. What happens among individuals, may happen in a complex society or political body.

The first application of the industry of men must be to procure the necessaries of life; by agriculture to supply themselves with food; by simple manufactures to furnish themselves with cloaths; by surrounding their towns with walls, to defend themselves from sudden attacks; and by establishing laws, to secure their property, and the peaceable enjoyment of the fruits of their labour. When some progress is made in these articles, and when human ingenuity has found out methods of facilitating labour, by which one man can do a great deal more than is necessary

sary to supply his own wants, and thus some of the society become exempted from corporeal toil, the human mind, stimulated by a love of excelling and being distinguished, begins to think of improvements, and to add what is convenient to what is necessary; 'till at last the views of men being extended, and their genius and taste refined, the elegancies and pleasures of life come to be thought of, the productions of men of superior talents are sought after, poems are read with pleasure, and pictures and statues are beheld with delight.

Navigia atque agri culturas, mœnia, leges,
Arma, vias, vestes, & cætera de genere horum,
Præmia, delicias, quoque vitæ funditùs omnes,
Carmina, picturas & dædala signa polire,
Usus & impigræ simul experientia mentis,
Paulatim docuit pedetentim progredientes;
Sic unum quicquid paulatim protrahit ætas
In medium, ratioque in luminis eruit oras:

Namque

Namque aliud ex alio clarefcere corde videmus
Artibus ad fummum donec venere cacumen *.

I could not forbear tranfcribing thefe lines from a poet of a moft original and beautiful genius, whofe work, though the main principles of his favorite fyftem are the moft abfurd imaginable, will be an immortal proof to what perfection poetry was brought among the Romans, by one who died before Octavius was born, or Julius Cæfar created perpetual dictator.

ONE indeed muft be little acquainted with the Hiftory of the beft Roman writers, who does not know that the nobleft compofitions which Rome ever produced, were the works of thofe who were born in the days of freedom. I fhall name only a few of the moft eminent of them; writers, who, by the concurring teftimony of all good judges, have been allowed to be the moft perfect and finifhed in their different ways.

* Lucret. Lib. 5.

I HAVE already taken notice of Lucretius, the greatest of all didactive poets. I ought to have mentioned before him, because he was prior in time, Terence, the beautiful simplicity and elegant correctness of whose compositions have always been admired. The works of this writer, while those of other comic wits fall into oblivion and disrepute with the modes and fashionable follies of the times for which they were wrote, will still be read and admired while men are men, or the great strokes of human characters continue to be the same. Terence died an hundred and ten years before the battle of Pharsalia.

SALUST the Historian, and Catullus the poet, whose great merit in their different ways is so well known, and so little disputed, that to do any more than name them would be an unnecessary task, were born much about the same time, thirty eight years before the battle of Pharsalia, as is commonly thought, and were both dead before the victory at Actium.

LETTER VI.

Actium had established the empire of Augustus.

HORACE was eighteen years of age at the time of the battle of Pharsalia; he was sent to Rome by his father when he was young, and had an education equally liberal with those who were of a much higher rank;

----Puerum est ausus Romam portare docendum
Artes quas doceat quivis eques, atque senator
Semet prognatos. --------

From the genteel manner in which he was taken care of, as appears from the lines, that immediately follow those I have just now transcribed, we may naturally suppose he was upon a footing of equality with the most liberal of the Roman youth, and in such society had his heart warmed with a love of freedom, and with such principles as afterwards made him appear at the battle of Philippi among the friends of Brutus and of liberty*.

* See Shaft. Advice to an author.

VIRGIL

VIRGIL was about five years older than Horace, and in all probability educated in the same principles; though, peaceful and gentle in his difpofitions, we do not find that he took up arms againft Octavius.

LIVY, it muft be acknowledged, wrote his Hiftory during the reign of Auguftus, and even furvived that emperor about four years; but as he died in an advanced age, in his feventy fixth year, the republic may claim the honour of having educated and formed this mafterly Hiftorian, fince he muft have been twenty eight years old, when the victory of Actium put an end to the refiftance that was made to Octavius, and fully eftablifhed his fupreme power. Unfortunately, indeed, that part of his Hiftory, which related the noble ftruggles in defence of liberty, during the laft period of the republic, is loft; but from the teftimony given of it, in the works of another great Hiftorian, we may eafily conceive the fpirit it breathed.----This elegant and candid writer, though he enjoyed a fhare of the friendfhip, which Auguftus had the prudence to fhow to all the great geniufes who flourifhed in his time, yet was true to the caufe of liberty. He was fo far from branding the names of Brutus and Caffius with the odious appellations of robbers and parricides, which were afterwards given them out of flattery to the emperors, that he often mentioned them as illuftrious men, and beftowed fuch praifes on Pompey, that Auguftus ufed to call him a Pompeian*.

The birth of Ovid and Tibullus is commonly fuppofed to have been in that year, when Hirtius and Panfa were confuls; and Propertius is thought to have been born a few years before. Some people indeed imagine, they have probable reafons to conclude that Tibullus was born twenty years before that

---

* Titus Livius elcquentiæ et fidei præclarus in primis, Cn. Pompeium tantis laudibus tulit, ut *Pompeianum* eum Auguftus appellaret: neque id amicitiæ eorum offecit. Scipionem, Affranium, hunc ipfum Caffium, hunc Brutum nufquam *latrones et Parricidas*, quæ nunc vocabula imponuntur, fæpe ut infignes viros nominat.
  Tacit. Ann. Lib. 4.

period;

period; if so, more than half his life was spent, when Rome was yet free. But even bringing his birth down as low as that of his friend Ovid, this triumvirate of poets and friends, whose works, written with true elegance, will be admired in every polished age, were born, while Julius Cæsar was still alive, and so far from having any reason to be real and hearty friends to Augustus, that they had much cause of resentment against him. Tibullus and Propertius, born and educated among those who strenuously opposed the lawless attempts of Octavius, must have imbibed in their most tender years a love of liberty, and hatred to Augustus. 'Tis probable that the father of Tibullus was killed fighting against Octavius, and that his estate became a prey to the rapacious soldiers. 'Tis the common opinion that the father of Propertius was one of those three hundred Roman citizens, whom Augustus, after he had taken Perusia, and they had surrendered to his mercy, inhumanly sacrificed at the altar of Julius, and to whose petitions for pardon, and apologies for their conduct, he made no other answer than this, *They must die**. That Propertius lost his fortune too, in the cause of freedom, is apparent from his works †.

Though Ovid never bore arms against Augustus, and wished him well, as he himself informs us ‡, when few of his country-

---

*. Perusiâ captâ, in plurimos animadvertit, orare veniam vel excusare se conantibus una voce occurrens, *moriendum esse*. Scribunt quidam trecentos ex dedititiis electos utriusque ordinis ad aram divo Julio extructam idibus Martiis mactatos.   Suet. in Aust.

To this Propertius himself probably alludes in the last Elegy of his first Book.

> Si Perusina tibi patriæ sunt nota sepulchra
>   Italiæ duris funera temporibus,
> Cum Romana suos egit discordia cives;
>   Sit mihi præcipuè pulvis Etrusca dolor.
> Tu projecta mei perpessa es membra propinqui
>   Tu nullo miseri contegis ossa solo.

† Nam tua cum multa versarent rura juvenci,
  Abstulit excultas pertica tristis opes. Lib. 4. Eleg. 1.

‡ —————— Nec contraria dicor
  Arma, nec hostiles esse secutus opes.
Optavi peteres cœlestia sidera tardé,
  Parsque fuit turbæ parva precantis idem.
       Ovid. Trist. Lib. 2.

men did so, yet he incurred the displeasure of the emperor, and without being allowed to stand a trial before the senate*, or any proper judge, was banished to a distant and disagreeable country. His offence yet remains a secret, but that it was rather a fault than a crime is highly probable: the punishment he suffered was therefore certainly severe, as well as arbitrary, and notwithstanding Augustus's boasted lenity, Ovid was very little obliged to him.

If to the celebrated names of Terence, Lucretius, Salust, Catullus, Virgil, Horace, Livy, Ovid, Propertius and Tibullus, we add those of Tully and Julius Cæsar himself, the admired list of the geniuses of what is called the Augustan age, will be compleat; for though the names of many, and some small pieces or fragments of several others, are handed down to us, yet those I have mentioned are

---

* Nec mea decreto damnasti facta senatus,
  Nec mea, selecto judice, jussa fuga est. Ibid.

the principal, and to their luftre 'tis owing that the age, in which they lived, fhines, and will for ever fhine forth with fuch diftinguifhed brightnefs in the annals of mankind.

It may feem odd that I mention Julius Cæfar among thofe writers who were formed by freedom, and who are quoted as examples of the happy influence of liberty upon elegance and tafte, fince he himfelf overthrew the free conftitution of his country. But though Cæfar, pufhed on by ambition and a too violent love of power, by force of arms became perpetual dictator, and trampled upon the conftitution of his country, his tafte was formed and corrected by freedom. 'Twas liberty, 'twas the talents neceffary to make one become eminent and powerful in a free ftate, 'twas the ftruggles which Cæfar had in his youth with a multitude of free and illuftrious antagonifts, and the ambition he had to excel in every thing, that formed his genius, his tafte, and thofe various abilities, which, unfortunately for freedom itfelf, enabled

bled him to get the better of all opposition; and make himself master of the republic.

No sooner were the Romans subjected to the arbitrary will of an emperor, than the genius and taste of Rome were at a stand. The protection Augustus gave to the great geniuses, who were formed in the time of liberty, and who flourished when fortune raised him to imperial sway, prevented, indeed, for some time, the bad effects, that his power naturally had upon taste from becoming apparent. From the sketch I have given, you see that the Augustan age was rendered immortal by those, who were born before that period; nay, that one half of the great writers I have mentioned died before ever the name of Augustus was heard of in the world: for among them, I may reckon Tully and Cæsar, the last of whom only saw him a mere boy, and the first was cruelly put to death, when Octavius was yet no more than an ambitious youth, associated with others for the destruction of freedom; but 'twas not till sixteen years after the death of Cicero, that he he assumed the title of Augustus, and the supreme dominion of the Roman empire. However, I do not know how it happens, that, people include, though 'tis very inaccurate, in the catalogue of writers of the Augustan age, all the fine geniuses of the last age of the republic.

If we reflect upon the shortness of that period which intervened from the first dawnings of elegance and taste among the Romans, till the destruction of their liberty, and consider that their genius and taste were at their greatest perfection, when they lost their freedom; and could never afterwards be equalled by any of those who were born in the times of slavery; we must be convinced that the decay of genius was owing to the loss of freedom, and be obliged to confess the intimate connection which subsists between liberty and true taste. The power of Augustus was so far from creating genius, or correcting taste, that it certainly put a stop to their improvement. Perhaps the very authors who wrote in his time, but were born

in

in the days of the republic, would have been more perfect, had they not survived the ruins of liberty. I cannot indeed conceive the lyre to have been touched with more exquisite Art, than it was by Horace; but had Virgil wrote before Rome was subjected to an imperial Lord, his compositions would perhaps have been animated with a nobler fire, and his own majesty might have been united with all the original spirit of Homer.

Horace observes, that the Roman genius, sublime and lively, was naturally well enough calculated for tragedy; but from the account he gives of their own tragedians, it appears that they were far from being perfect, and that though they discovered some beauties, yet these were tarnished by abundance of faults. Their translations from the Greek too, as he informs us in the same place, were not sufficiently correct *.

To

---
* ———————————— Quærere cœpit
Quid Sophocles, et Thespis, et Æschylus utile ferrent.
Tentavit quoque rem, si dignè vertere posset;
Et placuit sibi, naturâ sublimis et acer;

Nam

To what cause then shall we ascribe this fact, that among the Roman classics we meet with no tragedian that we can compare with the Grecian Æschylus, Sophocles, or Euripides? indeed that we meet with none at all of the classic age? for those which they had, have not been preserved from the ruins of time; but from the character given of them by the best judges among the Romans themselves, we may be certain that they were infinitely inferior to the Greek tragedians. This remarkable deficiency, this want of tragic writers among the Roman classics, can only be accounted for by ascribing it to the alteration, which was made in the constitution of Rome; a period was put to the liberty of the Romans, at the very time, when, by the natural progress of improvement, they would, if they had continued free, have excelled in tragedy. " A perfect tragedy is the noblest " production of human nature," to use the

Nam spirat tragicum satis, et feliciter audet;
Sed turpem putat in scriptis metuitque lituram.
                                        Epist. Lib. 2.

words of Mr. Addison.* What is best and noblest cannot be first, but must come last, and be produced among those who are already accomplished. Sophocles and Euripides were preceded by Homer; and, had the Romans continued longer free, Virgil would have been followed by tragedians worthy of the high Roman spirit, and the Latin tongue might have boasted of writers in that way, very different from a Seneca †, who wrote after Rome had been fully enslaved, her genius decayed, and her taste corrupted.

In vain do we look among the Romans, after this, for writers equal to those of the Ciceronian age. "Sint Mecænates, non dee-
" runt, Flacce, Marones ‡, may do very well in an epigram, but it will not be found to answer in fact. The liberty, the spirit, and knowledge of an age, must form the genius and taste of the writers of that age. 'Twas not owing to the patronage of Mecænas that Virgil was

* Spectator, No. 39. † Not the philosopher.
‡ Martial.

such

such an excellent poet, or to the want of such patrons that none comparable to him appeared afterwards. The noble genius, that dwelt among the free citizens of Rome, difdained to inhabit an enflaved country, or to attend upon the fubjects of a defpotic emperor. The protection, that Mecænas gave the fine writers, who flourifhed when he became minifter of the Roman empire, hath indeed rendered his name immortal, and made the generality of people believe that he was a man of tafte, the very reverfe of which is true: for as he was the firft minifter of arbitrary power, fo he gave the firft example among the Romans of the fatal influence of defpotifm upon tafte, by his own vitiated compofitions. Had Rome remained free, he perhaps might have been a great pattern of Roman eloquence, but too much profperity and luxury corrupted his tafte, unnerved his genius, and rendered his compofitions quite unmanly. "Ingeniofus "vir ille fuit, magnum exemplum Romanæ "eloquentiæ daturus, nifi illum enervaffet, "felicitas, imo, caftraffet," as Seneca fays of him in his nineteenth epistle*. Thus the first minister of Augustus, notwithstanding all the favour of the emperor, notwithstanding all his ambition to be reckoned a man of wit

* Besides what is quoted above, there are many passages in Seneca, which demonstrate the bad taste of Mecænas.

These lines of his which he cites Epist. 101.

> Debilem facito manu
> Debilem pede, coxâ;
> Tuber adstrue gibberum,
> Lubricos quate dentes;
> Vita dum superest, bene est.
> Hanc mihi vel acutâ
> Si sedeam cruce, sustine.

Are wretched, and demonstrate that his pretended admiration of Virgil must have been mere affectation. The author of these lines could never sincerely admire the *Usque adeone mori miserum est*, of that poet. Indeed, as Seneca says, one would hardly think he had ever heard Virgil recite this line. Shakespear, who never makes one speak out of character, has put similar sentiments in the mouth of a coward, who was willing to purchase life by a sacrifice of his sister's virtue.

The

wit and genius, and notwithstanding nature had originally endued him with a considerable share of parts, became an unchaste finical writer, and gave a striking proof, how little

> The wearieſt and moſt loathed worldly life,
> Which age, ach, penury, impriſonment,
> Can lay on Nature, is a paradiſe,
> To what we fear of death.
> Meaſure for Meaſure.

Seneca, in his 114th Epiſtle, after having given a ſpecimen of the obſcure, involved, licentious ſtyle of Mecænas, ſhews at great length, how it aroſe from his character and circumſtances. Hoc iſtæ ambages compoſitionis, hoc verba tranſverſa, hoc ſenſus magni quidem ſæpe, ſed enervati dum exeunt, cuivis manifeſtum facient, motum illi felicitate nimia caput; quod vitium hominis eſſe interdum, interdum temporis ſolet. See alſo Epiſt. 92. at the end. The calamiſtra (Curling Irons) of Mecænas are taken notice of by the author of the dialogue on the cauſes of the decay of Roman eloquence. How infinitely inferior are ſuch falſe ornaments to the ſimple dreſs of genuine eloquence! One would rather chooſe that an orator ſhould wear the rougheſt garb, than the gaudy and vitious dreſs of luxury and effeminacy. Malim herculè C. Gracchi impetum, aut L. Craſſi maturitatem, quam calamiſtros Mecænatis aut tinnitus Gallionis, adeo malim oratorem vel hirta toga induere, quam fucatis et meretriciis veſtibus inſignire.

influence the favour of Auguftus, even when moft lavifhly beftowed, could have in promoting genius or correcting tafte.

Augustus indeed perceived, and ufed to ridicule the effeminate and affected ftyle of his favourite*, yet he himfelf fell into a manner no lefs vitiated. Letters written with his own hand, as Suetonius informs us, difcovered what ridiculous phrafes he made ufe of; and how foppifhly he attempted to alter fome words. To exprefs the velocity of any thing done in a hurry, by faying *it was done more quickly than afparagus is boiled*, was undoubtedly fomething the very reverfe of the fublime; to exhort one to bear prefent calamities, by faying, *let us bear this Cato*, was certainly a wretched conceit, and yet thefe were the phrafes of Auguftus †. There is

---

* Exagitabat nonnunquam in primis Mecænatem fuum, cujus myrobrecheis (ut ait) concinnos ufquequaque perfequitur, et imitando per Jocum irridet.
      Suet. in Vit. Auguft. Cap. 86.

* Cum hortatur ferenda effe præfentia qualiacunque fint, contenti fimus hoc Catone, et ad exprimendam
      L   feftinatæ

is something very remarkable in the last of them: the awful name of Cato must have been extremely odious to him, and the remembrance of his virtues disagreeable. The glorious struggles of this brave citizen, in defence of freedom and virtue, must have reminded him of his own baseness in betraying both. Nothing can be more insupportable to such men as Augustus than characters like that of Cato: hence the origin of this phrase, which, as phrases often do, betrays the secret and heart-felt sentiments of its author. Such a baneful influence had the spirit of slavery upon its first great patrons among the Romans. An intimate familiarity with such men might have corrupted, but could never improve, the taste of any one. Nothing can be more absurd and trifling, than to ascribe the merit of the fine writers of those times to the patronage of the emperor or his mi-

---

festinatæ rei velocitatem, velocius quam asparagi coquantur: ponit assiduè pro stulto baceolum, et pro pullo, puleiaceum, et pro cerito vicerosum, et vapidè sese habere, pro malè, et betizare pro languere, &c.

Suet. in Aug. Cap. 87.

nister.

nister. They knew well how to make a proper use of those geniuses who then flourished, but who had been formed in other times and by conversation with different men. Taste was at its greatest height in Rome when Augustus came to the helm of affairs, and from that moment began to decline. 'Twas not all at once indeed extinguished; human society and the genius of men must be polished or made barbarous by degrees. But as the Romans, from the period when they began to be civilized, had made the most rapid progress in taste; and, in all probability, would have attained to a far greater degree of perfection, at least in some branches, had not the absolute power of the emperors checked their genius; so, from the time that a period was put to their liberty, they as rapidly declined, and the fatal effects of the change of their constitution upon taste became visible. Some writers appeared indeed, in the days of the emperors, of extraordinary merit. They were however few in number, and lived not in a period so distant from the Ciceronian age, but that we may naturally suppose, the noble spirit of that age might have been communicated to them, and the animating genius of liberty not yet altogether extinguished in Roman breasts.

In a dialogue, thought by some to have been written by Tacitus, but, as others think, by Quintilian, one of the speakers observes, that he does not know, why Cæsar and Cicero should rather be classed among the antient orators, than among those of their times, since the same person might have heard Cicero, and been present also at some of their own orations. He indeed brings the example of a man, who lived to a great age; but certainly the orations which the speakers in that dialogue made in their youth, might have been heard by one who had been present when Tully spoke, and they might all have been formed under those, who lived some time in the Ciceronian age *.

THUS,

---

* Sed Ciceronem et Cæsarem, &c.————cur antiquis temporibus potius adscribatis quam nostris non video. Nam ut de Cicerone ipso loquar, Hirtio nempe
et

Thus, the age of Tacitus, so far from being very distant from that of Cicero, may in some measure be reckoned the same; and in this age flourished the last of the great Roman authors; for Quintilian, the Pliny's, and Juvenal were cotemporary with him. After this, even all the favour of emperors, who were both good men and great philosophers, could *not* keep up the antient spirit,

et Pansa consulibus, ut Tiro libertus ejus scribit VII. Idus Decemb. occisus est, quo anno Divus Augustus in locum Pansæ et Hirtii se et Q. Pedium coss. suffecit. Statue VI et L annos, quibus mox divus Augustus remp. rexit: adjice Tiberii XXIII. et prope quadriennium Caii, ac bis quaternos denos Claudii et Neronis annos, atque ipsum Galbæ et Othonis, et Vitellii unum annum, ac VI. jam felicis hujus principatûs stationem qua Vespasianus remp. fovet. C et XX anni, ab interitu Ciceronis in hunc diem colliguntur, unius hominis ætas. Nam ipse ego in Britannia vidi senem, qui se fateretur et pugnæ interfuisse, qua Cæsarem inferentem arma Britanniæ, arcere littoribus, et pellere agressi sunt: ita si eum, qui armatus C. Cæsari restitit, vel captivitas, vel voluntas, vel fatum aliquod in urbem pertraxisset, idem Cæsarem ipsum et Ciceronem audire potuit et nostris quoque actionibus interesse.

Dialog. de Cauf. Corrupt. Eloquent.

or produce writers comparable to those of the days of freedom.

Despotism and a false taste seem to have gone hand in hand, 'till both appeared in their genuine colours. Some appearances were kept up in the days of Augustus: even in the days of Tiberius there were some remains of dying liberty, " manebant etiam " tunc vestigia morientis libertatis," as Tacitus says in the first Book of his Annals. The good emperors, who came after those monsters that succeeded Tiberius, revived the drooping spirit of the Romans, and in their time we meet with some useful writers, but of a taste much inferior to that of the age of freedom. As despotism approached, taste and genius retired from among the Romans, till at last we do not even meet with a faint resemblance of what they once were; freedom of spirit gave way to mean flattery, noble ideas to wretched conceits, a simple and nervous style to a florid unmanly one, and a severe correctness to a relish for whatever was vitious, tawdry or foppish.

Thus,

Thus, my Lord, I have endeavoured to answer the arguments that may be brought for the superior advantages, which taste is by some people thought to have in an absolute government, from the common opinion about the influence of the protection which Augustus afforded the muses. By a short sketch I have shewn that the last age of the republic formed the great writers of the Augustan age, that the emperor's power put a stop to farther improvement, that, in all probability, had the Romans continued longer free, they would have arrived at a much higher degree of perfection, at least in some branches, and that arbitrary power and bad taste gained ground at the same time, till at last despotism was fully established, and taste thoroughly depraved.

I intended to have answered the objections which are brought from the age of Lewis XIV. but this I must delay: the present letter has been much longer than I thought it would have been, but I shall make no apology, as 'tis

'tis wrote in vindication of the honours which juftly belong to freedom, and in defence of her caufe, a caufe which I hope you will ever revere in your heart and fupport by your conduct.

I am, &c.

LETTER VII.

On the INFLUENCE of LIBERTY upon TASTE, and of the Age of LEWIS XIV.

My Lord,

EVERY gentleman ought to build his opinion of nations, of men, and of the different ages of the world, upon rational principles; one ought however especially to be careful to reason justly with respect to those ages which have certainly been the most accomplished, and from which, maxims will often be drawn, and examples brought of whatever is most hurtful or beneficial to mankind. I have endeavoured to shew in a former letter how far the common opinion with regard to the influence of Augustus's power upon genius and taste is unjust, and how much the generality of people, misled by the delicate flattery paid to him and Mecænas by writers formed in the days of liberty, but who survived the republic, and were the greatest ornaments of the court of Augustus, have mistaken the real genius of this emperor and his minister, and the influence of their power upon true taste. I shall now offer you some observations concerning the age of Lewis XIV. They are such as have occurred to me in reading the celebrated writers and historians of that age.

Persuaded of the truth of this general proposition, that in proportion as a country is free, true taste will flourish, unless the happy influence of freedom be counterbalanced by other unfavourable circumstances, and that the protection of no single man can create genius or taste, which must be formed by the peculiar circumstances of the nation and age in which men of taste and genius appear; I am convinced sufficient reasons may be given for the figure which the French writers of of the age of Lewis XIV. make, and will for ever make in the annals of the world, without having recourse to the influence of his supreme power, or drawing a conclusion unfavourable to liberty. If I shall not be so happy as to point out the circumstances which enabled the fine geniuses of France in that age to adorn their works with so much elegance and correctness, without ascribing it principally to the patronage which their monarch gave to the sciences and arts, your Lordship must impute it to my want of skill, and not to the badness of the argument which I endeavour to support.

It hath often been observed that there was a great resemblance between the courts of Augustus and Lewis, and that many similar circumstances contributed to immortalize the reigns of both. A great deal of common-place flattery has been most lavishly offered up, and virtues and talents ascribed to both, which perhaps neither of them had any title to lay claim to.

But

But that they were both fortunate, is undoubtedly true. The nobleſt fortune that an emperor or king can attain to, is to become ſovereign of a people at a time when they are eminent for their accompliſhments, for the illuſtrious figure they make in the world, and for the improvements they have made in whatever can tend to embelliſh life, or render ſociety more rational and polite. Such were the Romans and French, when Auguſtus and Lewis came to ſupreme power. Rome had produced her Lucretius, Salluſt, Cicero! Paris had produced her Corneille, Molliere, Paſcal! I have mentioned theſe three, becauſe it is allowed by every one, that both the French poetry and proſe were carried by them to a degree of elegance and perfection perhaps unequalled, but certainly not excelled by any, who have appeared ſince their time, and becauſe the youngeſt of them (Paſcal) was born fifteen years before Lewis, and publiſhed his famous Provincials when that prince was only ſixteen years of age, and cannot be ſuppoſed to have had any influence

fluence in forming or promoting a good taste in France.

It may indeed be said, and with much appearance of reason too, what is this to the purpose, and how does this shew that an arbitrary government is unfriendly to taste? since 'tis equally the same, whether these writers were born in the time of Lewis XIV. or in that of the kings his predecessors. But, my Lord, 'tis not the same. I shall endeavour to shew that the period, when the French taste was gradually improving, and attained to such perfection, was a period when real liberty was gaining ground; when, though the kings of France became more powerful, the rights of the bulk of the people were enlarged, their spirits animated, and a desire of knowledge and a freedom of inquiry highly prevalent in France.

It does not follow that in proportion as the powers of the sovereign are encreased, the people become slaves: That nation is

most

most free where most people are free, to use words which, I have heard it said, were spoke by a man of great learning and experience upon a bill to take away certain jurisdictions, that prevented the happy influence of freedom from reaching to the remote parts of this island. The kings of France had for a long period of years been endeavouring to overthrow that system which put it in the power of a few great men to despise their sovereign, to throw their country into confusion, whenever their pride prompted them to it, and to trample upon the generality of the people. The methods which those monarchs found it necessary to take to establish their own authority, happily for the bulk of the people, were calculated in some measure to promote their independence and liberty.

The administration of justice is of the highest consequence in every country. They who have it in their power to determine concerning the lives and property of the people must

must have the highest authority, and if they are not obliged to judge according to a certain system of law, but as their own wills dictate, must become arbitrary and despotic. Such were the great Lords in France during the prevalence of the Feudal government: Leaders and captains in the fields; they were supreme judges in time of peace, and, by having every thing in their disposal, were the absolute and uncontroulable masters of the people who could have recourse to none but them for the preservation or recovery of their property, and thus were indeed their mere slaves. ------ " Ce n'etoit plus des subjets,
" que des peuples qui pouvoient être armés
" contre le roi par leur seigneurs, et qui,
" pour conserver leur bien, ne connoissoient
" d'autre Tribunal que celui de ce même
" seigneur*," a short but an accurate and comprehensive description of the feudal system. To appoint judges, who should take cognizance of the determinations of those tribunals, redress the grievances of the people,

* Henaut. Remarques sur la troisieme race.

and

and judge according to law, was at once to free the commons from oppression, to extend the power of the sovereign, and to establish a regular system of laws; in a word, 'twas to diffuse liberty among the bulk of the people, and, as Mr. Voltaire in his lively manner expresses it, to give five hundred thousand families reason to rejoice at what perhaps fifty murmured *.

That this was the method the kings of France actually took, you will be convinced by reading their histories; particularly the concise and accurate one of Henaut, every page of which will instruct you, and enlarge your ideas, especially on this subject. I have only taken notice of this alteration of the French government in general, because 'tis an illustrious proof that liberty is friendly to genius and taste, since that period, in which the French

* C'est à lui (Louis XI.) que le peuple doit le premier abaisement des grands. Environs cinquante familles en ont murmuré, et plus de cinq cens milles dû s'en feliciter.   Hist. Gener. Louis XI.

were making a gradual progress in learning and politeness, was also a period in which freedom was gaining ground, and the bulk of the people emerging from the meanest servitude. In this period parliaments were established, and judges appointed, who by degrees became more and more respectable, able to defend the people from oppression, the awful dispensers of justice, and the guardians of law. The noble and generous struggles, which the parliaments of France, particularly that of Paris, have lately, and for many years past, made in defence of the fundamental laws of their country, have merited and obtained the applause of all Europe*, and made it no rash assertion to affirm that their institution and growing power hath been a favourable circumstance to the liberty of France.

* Le parlement de Paris, s'est conduit depuis pres de deux ans avec une fermité et une prudence qui lui on valu des remercimens du prince, l'affection de tous les bons François, et l'estime de toute l'Europe.

Mes Pensées.

BUT

But not only had the alteration which was made in the administration of justice an influence to enlarge the freedom of the people; that which was made in military affairs had the same effect, and equally tended to promote taste. While the feudal system prevailed, the Great, retired in sullen pride, shut up in their gloomy castles, defended by their vassals and slaves, and entertained by martial feats, by tournaments and savage combats, were utterly ignorant of every thing that was elegant and polite. When they had taken the field against a neighbouring rival, or appeared with their vassals in the general army of their country, they returned as soon as war was at an end to their own domains, accompanied with their followers, and never lived at court or among their equals. Flattered by, and proudly dictating to, their inferiors, 'tis easy to conceive what an influence this must have had to encourage the Great in their follies, to debase the minds of the people, and to prevent both from making any improvements in knowledge or taste.

By

By destroying this system, the bulk of the people were freed from a perpetual and servile attendance upon their superiors; the Great, having less employment at home, were attracted to court *, their Taste was changed, genteel amusements took place of rougher exercises, themselves and their country were gradually improved, reading became fashionable, and society grew more rational and polite. In vain were these improvements attempted to be made, during the continuance of the Feudal system, a system, of all others, the least friendly to the fine arts, or to the liberties of the bulk of mankind, which are always connected. Kings in vain encouraged letters: in vain did Charles V. of France collect a library of nine hundred Volumes, a great number before the art of printing was invented: the genius of his country was against him, and defeated the influence of that protection and encouragement he gave to learning and arts †. The liberality of princes

* Hen. Rem. sur la troisieme race.
† Le roi de France Charles V. qui rassembla environs 900 Volumes, cens ans avant que la Bibliotheque du

princes can have but a very small effect, in promoting genius or taste, among a people whose minds are debased by servitude. The kings of France, by destroying the Feudal system, and thus altering the genius of the people, and giving spirits to the minds of men, did more to promote knowledge and taste, than all the rewards and protection, that could be given to the learned and ingenious, before that system was overturned, could possibly do.

Francis I. whose reign is the great epoch of the revival of letters in France, did not hold learning in higher esteem, or more liberally encourage science and arts than Charles V. whose memorable answer to one that murmured at the honours which he shewed to men of learning, " Science and " the learned cannot be too much honour- " ed ; while learning is honoured in this

du Vatican fut fondée par Nicolas V. encouragea en vain les talents : le terrain n'etoit pas preparé pour porter de ces fruits etrangers.
Volt. tom. 2d. See also Henaut Charles V.

" king-

"kingdom, it will continue in prosperity, but "when it shall be despised, the kingdom "will decline and fall *," ought for ever to be remembered with applause. But the genius of their times was different: the one lived before, and the other after, Lewis XI. who, though a bad man and a cruel prince, laid a foundation for the improvements of arts and sciences, by freeing the bulk of the people from that dependence and servitude in which they were kept, during the prevalence of the Feudal system.

ANOTHER memorable event, that happened about a century before the birth of Lewis XIV. must have had the greatest influence to animate the minds of men, and give a spur to genius; I mean the reformation, an event intimately connected with a spirit of liberty,

---

* Quelq' un murmuroit de l'honeur qu'il portoit aux gens des lettres, appellés dans ces tems *clercs*; il respondit; *les clercs, ou la sapience*, l'on ne peut trop honorer; et tant que sapience sera honoreé en ce royaume, il continuera en prosperité, mais quand deboutée y'sera, il decherra. *Henault.*

and a freedom of enquiry. In a letter, which I wrote to you some time ago, I took notice of the happy influence this had upon human affairs, and the liberties of Europe in general*. I shall at present only observe, that, in no country, where the reformation did not actually take place, were the protestants more numerous or considerable than in France. Men of the most eminent abilities, who made a figure in the cabinet, and in the field, several princes of the blood, and many of the *noblesse*, as well as a vast number of the commons, were of the protestant party. The struggles which they made in their own defence, and which were often successful; the disputes which they had with the catholics, not only in the way of arms, but of argument and debate, could not fail of having a considerable effect to enlarge the understandings of men, to correct their judgments, and to inspire their imaginations and fancies, with a vivacity and justness, to be acquired only by practice, and by being often put to the

* See page 41, 42, 43, 47, 48, 49.

necessity

necessity of defending favourite, or of attacking odious opinions, by being warmly interested, and by having an occasion of exercising every faculty of the human mind, and power of the human body, in defence of ourselves, our country, or our friends.

This naturally leads me to take notice of a circumstance which certainly had the greatest influence to form the ages both of Augustus and Lewis. I mean, the civil wars and contentions, to which they succeeded. What an exertion of great talents must there have been in Rome, when the Catos, the Ciceros, the Pompeys, the Cæsars, and the Antonys, were at the head of different parties, and, with all their abilities, endeavouring to support their own, or to weaken that of their enemy's! What a noble struggle must it have been in France, when the Henrys*, the Sullys, the de Mornays, the Condés, the Turennes, the De Retzs, the Rochefoucaults, the Richlieus, and the Ma-

* Henry IV.

zarins, drew their swords and made use of their eloquence to support the interests of contending parties, and to defend the principles of opposite systems *.

Thus, my Lord, I have endeavoured to prove that in France, during the reigns of several kings preceding Lewis XIV. the rights of the bulk of the people were enlarged, their understandings improved by a freedom of enquiry, their spirits animated, and their taste made manly and bold by perpetual struggles about independence and freedom, both sacred and civil: in a word, that a spirit of liberty prevailed and formed those geniuses, who flourished when he came to the throne, and during the last years of his fa-

† Ces deux princes sortoient des guerres civiles, de ce tems, ou les peuples, toujours armées, nourris sans cesse au milieu des perils, entêtès des plus hardies deseins, ne voyent rien ou ils ne puissent atteindre, de ce tems au les evenements heureux et malheureux, mille fois repeteés, etendent les idees, fortifient l'ame a force d'Epreuves, augmentent son ressort, et lui donnent ce desir de gloire qui ne manque jamais de produire de grandes choses. *Henaut.*

ther's reign. I say, during the last years of his father's reign; for it is of importance to remember that, in the time of Richlieu's administration, genius and taste had attained to the highest perfection; an unanswerable proof, that a spirit of liberty, and the circumstances of the times, have a greater influence to form the great writers and artists of the times, than even the protection of a court and a minister, since some of the most eminent of them met with no encouragement either from the court or ministry, but rather the contrary.

The great Corneille received no favours from Richlieu; nay, 'tis well known that he met with opposition from him, and that too much complaisance to that minister made the academy condemn his famous *Cid*. But other circumstances tended to elevate his genius more than this could depress it. Born in an active and illustrious age, himself endued with great talents, and admired by men, to whom nature had been no less bountiful, need we wonder at the sublimity to which he attained?

tained? need we wonder at the grandeur of his sentiments, when we reflect upon the sensibility of his applauding audience? What an incitement must it have been to write well, to perceive a generous tear drop from the great Condé at the pronouncing of a noble and generous sentiment!*

A LITTLE anecdote concerning the manner in which the son of this Condé entertained Marshal Turenne, during a visit of two days, which he made to Chantilli, will give you a very different idea of the way in which the illustrious men of France were then regaled, from what is to be seen in more modern times, and make you easily perceive how great the taste for learning and fine compositions must have been in France at that time, and how natural it is to expect to meet with fine writers in an age, and among a people, whose manners were so polite, and whose

* Le grand Corneille faisant pleurer le grand Condé, d'admiration, est une époch bien célébre dans l'histoire de l'esprit humain. *Volt.*

entertainments were so rational and instructive. "The duke (son to the great Condé) "wanting to give an entertainment to M. "De Turenne in which nothing should be "omitted that could be agreeable to that "great general, consulted Mr. Despreaux "about what was most proper to read to "him. The satyrist (M. Despreaux) was "himself engaged to read three Cantos of his "Lutrin; but there were other vacant hours "to fill up, during those two days, when they "hoped to have the pleasure of entertaining "M. De Turenne. Despreaux proposed "to read the Provincial Letters, which the "duke had not seen. They read one of "them for a trial, which his highness was so "charmed with, that he took the book, and "could not leave off, 'till he had read them "all. M. De Turenne was no less delighted "with those letters, which he chose to hear "read again and again *." Does not this put us in mind of the symposiums of Greece, or

* See a discourse prefixed to the provincial letters. Paris, 1753.

of the taſte of thoſe ſocieties at Rome, to which old Cato often reſorted, and which he valued, not on account of exquiſite diſhes and rich wines, but of good company and ingenious converſation. " Neque enim ip-
" ſorum conviviorum delectationem volup-
" tatibus corporis, magis quam cætu amico-
" rum et ſermonibus metiebar *. When ſuch a taſte prevailed at Athens, Rome, and Paris, need we wonder that works were produced, which will render the ages, in which they were wrote, immortal ? need we wonder that among the great number of learned, high-ſpirited, and illuſtrious men in every way, with which France then abounded, there aroſe ſome, with geniuſes capable of reform-ing taſte, and of fixing its ſtandard, by pre-ſenting the public with elegant and noble models ? certainly we need not; nor need we be ſurpriſed that the ſublimity and genuine elegance of thoſe writers have not been ex-celled by any who have appeared ſince the ad-miniſtrations of Richlieu and Mazarin. By

* Tull. Cat. Maj.

reflecting upon the state of France, immediately before these ministers came to the helm of affairs, by considering their conduct and the alteration they made in the constitution of their country, the principle I have been endeavouring to establish, will be illustrated, and confirmed.

Henry IV. the best and most amiable of princes, who enjoyed the greatest happiness, that can fall to the share of a mortal, and which most resembles that of the Divinity, the heart-felt pleasure of making millions happy, of diffusing plenty and joy, and of using power to execute the dictates of goodness, was at once the sovereign and friend of his people. Intimately connected, when a prince of the blood, with the supporters of liberty; on the throne, he was the protector of freedom. Educated a Protestant, he continued after he became a Catholic to be the patron of the reformed, and his principal ministers were of that profession. Generous and free in his own principles, he endeavoured to promote a spirit of love and charity among his

his subjects, to allay all bitterness and animosity, and to put an end to all persecution. He called together the estates of his kingdom; not to force them to a compliance with his own will, nor to despise their counsels, but with a sincere intention to follow them. All his actions discovered a greatness of mind; all his words were the unfeigned pictures of a generous heart: posterity will for ever remember them with virtuous applause; with what emotions of gratitude then must they have inspired the breasts of his subjects, with what admiration must they have beheld his actions, and with what rapture must they have heard the benevolent expressions of his affectionate regard to the interests of his country, and of mankind in general! Such qualities would have appeared amiable at all times, but if you reflect upon the state of France for some years before Henry came to the throne, you will be convinced, that he must have appeared like an angel, sent from heaven to bless mankind; or, as the antients related of their Apollo, to inspire men with great and beautiful ideas, to make the voice of the

muses

muses be heard, by putting an end to the horrid noise of inhuman war; and to rescue the people from cruel famine,

> Hic bellum lacrymosum, hic miseram famem
> Pestemque a populo aget *.

THAT Henry came to the throne, at a time, when the French had been exposed to the most dreadful effects of these severest scourges of human kind, is well known. Not inspired by a generous principle of supporting their liberties and laws; or of defending their country against a foreign enemy, but instigated by inhuman superstition, the catholics of France had taken up arms to imbrue their hands in the blood of their fellow citizens. The massacre of Paris, and the famous siege of that city, which happened some years after, will be remembered as eternal proofs, what superstition can prompt its bigotted votaries to do, and suffer. Neither age, nor sex, nor beauty, nor merit, could make

* Hor.

the dagger fall from the hand of the barbarous affaffin: nor could a famine, fo dreadful as even to inftigate a wretched mother to eat her own child, oblige the Parifians to furrender their city to one whom they were taught to look upon as accurfed.

Henry, however, overcame every obftacle. 'Twas impoffible for the moft bigoted to keep up a *league* againft him, that could any longer prevent his afcending the throne. Happy was it for France that he became king. To the moft cruel and tumultuous fucceeded times the moft peaceful and generous. Secured in the poffeffion of their rights and privileges, and of every thing that they held moft dear, no one was any longer afraid of falling a victim to the cruelty of a bafe affaffin, or to the infolence of a haughty minion of power.

The minds of men, which had been agitated during the preceding reigns, and obliged to make ufe of every effort for felf-prefervation and defence, being now no longer
kept

kept in perpetual alarm, had leizure to apply that vigour and activity which they had acquired to the embellishment of life, and to the improvement of whatever was elegant and polite. What great things Henry did for the ease, the plenty, and security of his people, is well known; what more he might have done, had not an infamous wretch put an untimely period to his glorious career, may be conjectured from what he did. But that, during this reign of freedom and joy, a foundation was laid, for that high reputation the French afterwards acquired for genius and taste, which, as I observed before, appeared in their utmost lustre, during the administrations of Richelieu and Mazarin, cannot be doubted. Nor is it absurd to suppose, that, as the spirit of liberty, and the freedom, which prevailed in France before they came to the helm of affairs, contributed greatly to form the sublime taste of the illustrious writers of their times, so a check was given to farther improvement, by the large strides which they made towards arbitrary power.

EVERY body knows with what intrepid boldness the first, and with what consummate art the last of these ministers aggrandized the power of their masters, and paved the way to despotism.

Richelieu, Mazarin, ministres immortelles;
Jusqu' au Trone elevés de l'ombre des autels:
Enfans de la fortune et de la politique,
Marcheront a grands pas au pouvoir despo-
    tique *.

To enter minutely into the alterations which they made in the constitution of France would require more time than I can at present bestow upon it: besides, the fact is allowed on all hands, and there are not more or better helps for acquiring a thorough knowledge of the transactions of any country in any period, than of those of France at that time. The principal actors were men of great abilities every way, and being capable of writing, as well as of acting with spirit, the world

* Volt. Hen.

is furnished with ample materials to judge of the conduct of all parties, and to form their opinions from the accounts of those who were best acquainted with the transactions of the times. Your Lordship will be greatly instructed and amused with the original memoirs of that period; but that you may see how far the Constitution of France was then altered, and its liberty abridged, I shall give you the trouble to read some sentences, transcribed from eminent French writers, which in a few words will shew you what these alterations were, better than I could do, and at the same time prove the truth of what has been affirmed, that the French government at that period became more absolute than it had formerly been *.

I COULD

---

*. Ce ministre (Richelieu) dont la politique absoluë avoit violé les anciennes loix du royaume pour etablir l'authorité *immoderée* de son maitre, dont il etoit dispensateur; avoit consideré tous les reglemens de cet etat, comme des concessions forceés, et des bornes imposeés a la puissance des roys, plutot que de fondemens solides pour bien regner; et comme son administration tres

longue

I could produce a great many more authorities to prove what I have asserted, but these

longue avoit eté authorisée, par de grands succez pendant la vie du feu roy, il renversa toutes les formes de la justice et des finances, et avoit introduit pour la souverain tribunal de la vie et les bien des hommes, *la volonte royale.* Mem. de M. de la Rochefoucault.

Le Cardinal de Richelieu fit, pour ainsi dire, un fond de toutes les mauvaise intentions et de toutes les ignorance des deux derniers siecles, pour s'en servir selon ses interêts. Il les deguisa en maximes utiles et necessaires pour etablir l'autorité royale, et la fortune secondant ses desseins, par le desarmement du parti protestant en France, par les victoires des Suedois, par la foiblesse de l'empire, par l'incapacité d'Espagne, il forma dans la plus legitime des monarchies la plus scandaleuse et la plus dangereuse tyrannie, qui ait peut-être jamais asservi un etat. Mem. de Retz.

Il (Richelieu) fit un coup d'etat, en abbaissant les grands seigneurs, de maniere qu'il n'y on a plus aujourd-hui. Il fit un coup d'etat, en ôtant aux religionaires, leurs places de sureté. Il fit un coup d'etat en eloignant des affaires les princes du sang, et en les reduissant a la condition de simples sujets.

Mais

these are enough, and perhaps indeed more than enough: for your Lordship may possibly think that I have brought myself into a strange dilemma, either of denying that the French, since the times of Richelieu and Mazarin have been eminent for genius and taste, or of contradicting the principle I have taken so much pains to establish, that these cannot subsist in a despotic government. But I hope I am neither so partial, nor so utterly void of discernment, as not to allow the French of the present times to be conspicuous both for genius and taste; and I hope too, that I shall be able to account for it, consistently with my opinion about the influence of liberty.

It must be carefully remembered that the greatest geniuses the French can boast of, the Corneilles and Molieres, the Bossuets and

---

Mais n'etendoit-il pas, n'affermissoit-il assez par ces dispositions l'autorité royale ? etoit-il necessaire de la rendre absoluë ? ne precipita-t-il pas les choses d'un exces dans un autre ? n'altera-t-il pas la constitution fondamentale du royaume ?   *Mes Pensées.*

Rochefoucaults, the Pouffins and Le Bruns, and a great many more of their illustrious cotemporaries * were born before the efforts of Richelieu had fully established the power of the French monarchs, and were formed in times, when that minister had not as yet given, what Cardinal De Retz, in his animated manner, calls a movement of rapidity to the royal authority †.

Had Richelieu been followed by a succession of ministers, who, bold and successful as himself, had been able to make the torrent of royal power flow with increasing velocity,

---

* Corneille was born in 1606, Moliere in 1620. Bossuet in 1627. Rochefoucault in 1613. Pouffin in 1594. Le Brun in 1619. Richelieu may be said to have attained to the height of his power, after having reduced Rochelle in 1628, or rather after having defeated the intrigues against him, and got the better of all his antagonists in 1632.

† Le mouvement de rapidité que Mr. le Cardinal Richelieu avoit donné a l'autorité royale.
Mem. De Retz.

and

and sweep away every inferior obstacle with its impetuous stream, the French would indeed have become mere slaves, and genius and true taste would quickly have disappeared; but after his death they got a breathing time, and during the weakness of a minority, curbed the power of his successor, invested the magistrates and laws with somewhat of their former dignity, and shewed a spirit, that obliged Mazarin to leave the kingdom for some time, and made him, after his return, cautious how he meddled with the rights of a people, which he found had still some power and much inclination to oppose him. It required all his art not to suffer the crown to lose that power, which Richelieu had acquired: to increase or carry it further was an attempt beyond his courage or genius.

That Lewis XIV. was absolute cannot be denied; but he was so, more by his great *personal* character, and by the *voluntary* obedience that his *admiring* subjects paid him,

LETTER VII.

than by any alteration he made in the constitution beyond what Richelieu had done.

What the situation of France has been under his succeffor is well known. The firmnefs and integrity of the magiftrates hath given force and dignity to the laws; the prudent and feafonable remonftrances of the parliaments have fupported the credit of their body, and prevented great encroachments from being made upon the fundamentals of the conftitution, by a feeble adminiftration, and a prince whom even his friends will not pretend to be of an elevated or enterprifing character. When the members of the parliament of Paris were lately banifhed on account of the religious difputes, which have fo long prevailed in France, it was found impracticable to carry on the bufinefs of the nation by an arbitrary council fubftituted in their place. Without making conceffions, or giving up the point in difpute, they were recalled, and have fince, to their immortal honour, continued to defend the liberties of France,

France, and to punish those priests, who refuse the sacraments to such as will not declare their full assent to the constitution *Unigenitus*, by which these worthy magistrates have demonstrated that liberty is not entirely abolished in France.

THANK heaven, we in Great Britain are blest with a freedom unequalled by that of any other nation in the world. Of this happy freedom we have reason to boast, but we ought not rashly to pronounce that other nations are mere slaves, and to talk as if we made no distinction between the slavery of Turkey and France. They indeed must be utterly unacquainted with this latter country, who don't know, that among the French, justice is regularly administred, and private property secured by the guardians of the law, who are a great and respectable body, which they never are in a despotic government; and that though the inhabitants of France do not enjoy a freedom comparable to that of Britain, yet they are

certainly

certainly more free than the enflaved Afiatics, or even than feveral European nations.

The argument, upon the whole, may be fummed up in a few words. The period, in which the French tafte was gradually improving, was a period when the rights of the bulk of the people were gaining ground; genius and tafte were carried to their greateft perfection by thofe who were born at the very time when France was moft free. Since the adminiftration of Richelieu, the government hath been more arbitrary, and tafte hath not made any advances, perhaps hath not been kept up with an equal degree of elegance and fpirit. But though it fhould be allowed that it has, even this cannot greatly invalidate the argument in favour of the happy influence of liberty, fince the French are certainly not fo utterly deprived of freedom, or fo much oppreffed by the iron rod of flavery, as to be rendered incapable, like the fubjects of defpotic emperors, to be animated and improved by other favourable circumftances.

It would, indeed, be strangely unreasonable and bigotted to pretend, that liberty alone is sufficient to improve the taste of a nation, or that better opportunities, or more care may not make a people, that enjoys a smaller share of freedom, excel one which possesses a greater, but is not blest with equal advantages in other respects, or has not had its attention so long turned to objects of taste. There are degrees of freedom as of other things; every one is not endued with equally good parts; but pains and better opportunities often enable the man of *middling* talents to make a greater figure than one of far superior natural abilities, who wanted these opportunities, or made a bad use of such as he had. There is, however, a certain stupidity in some individuals, and despotism prevails so thoroughly in some countries, as to baffle every attempt to *improve*, or at least every effort to *excel*.

In a letter which I formerly wrote to your Lordship*, I took notice of some circum-

* See letter 5th.

stances

stances favourable to the taste of France, arising from the peculiar genius and situation of its metropolis; but there are also other advantages that the French in general enjoy, which, it can hardly be denied, must have a happy influence.

THEIR language has become almost the universal language of Europe: their productions are read, translated, approved of, or criticized every where: the best books of other nations too are translated into French: the most ingenious of all countries visit theirs, are desirous of becoming acquainted with their celebrated men, and of communicating their own sentiments to them. Though there are restraints upon the press at Paris, yet they fall upon ways of eluding them, or, if in some cases they fail, Holland supplies them with whatever they want, and books of all kinds may be procured in France: no country is better stored with them, and no where does reading more generally prevail.

IF

If 'tis univerfally allowed that the invention of printing, by making the noble productions of Greece and Rome be read by vaft numbers, contributed greatly to diffufe the genuine tafte and freedom of fpirit which began to prevail in the fixteenth century; may it not with equal reafon be owned, that the French, by having an opportunity of reading, in their own language, the beft works of every country, are poffeffed of great opportunities of improvement, and of having their minds enlarged, and their prejudices corrected? How many Frenchmen have been the pupils of Bacon, of Locke, and of other illuftrious geniufes, formed in this ifland, as well as in other free countries abroad? The univerfality of the French language hath almoft made the French, citizens of the world, and put it in their power to catch the fpirit, to imbibe the fentiments, and to acquire the ideas, which prevail among the ingenious men of every country.

It has alfo had another effect; it has opened an eafy accefs to Frenchmen into every country

country of Europe, and made the ingenious of that nation be well received every where; as people are fond of becoming acquainted with the eminent men of a country, which has so long acquired the lead in polite accomplishments, and whose language every court in Europe makes use of, when transacting business with foreign states. Conscious of this advantage, the free spirits of France are more independent at home than they would otherwise be, as they are sure of a retreat in foreign countries, if their freedom should happen to disoblige the governors of their own, or make it disagreeable for them to remain in France. When bigotry and envy had raised a party to get president Montesquieu debarred from those honours which his merit gave him a title to lay claim to, he told the ministry, that if such an injury should be done him, he would leave his native country, and accept of that security and those honours which foreigners liberally offered him*. This, in all probability,

---

* See an account of his life in the Encyclop.

bility, prevented his being excluded from the French academy, and emboldened him to write with still more freedom in his *spirit of laws*, than he had done in the *Persian letters*, which at that time gave offence.

In fact, do not we know that some of the greatest men, whom France can at present boast to have given birth to, live abroad, honoured and caressed? I need only name two of them, Maupertius * and Voltaire, the first of whom is at the head of his Prussian majesty's academy, and the second, hath at last fixed his abode in the territories of a free state, where independent, he lives beyond the reach of arbitrary power, inspired by that goddess eternally adored by mankind, the animating soul of every grand attempt, the object of noble vows, which, when present, every mortal with joy embraces, or, if absent, longs for and anxiously recalls, which lives in every heart, and whose

* Maupertius died since this letter was written.

sacred

sacred name is silently worshipped even in the courts of tyrants; By liberty---to borrow his own sentiments,

> -----C'est sur ces bords heureux
> Qu' habite des humains la deefs eternelle,
> L'aime des grands travaux, l'objet des noble voeux,
> Que tout mortel embrasse, ou desire, ou rapelle,
> Qui vit dans tous les cœurs, et dont le nom sacré
> Dans les cours des tyrans est tout bas adoré,
> La liberté.---------

Lines which I could not help transcribing from an admirable epistle, written by him, when he arrived at his Villa near the lake of Geneva.

THERE is a mighty difference between the state of Europe at present, and what it was, when the Roman emperors became masters of the world. Their sway was universal, their subjects could cast their eyes upon no neighbouring

bouring free country, where they might be sheltered from oppression, and a view of whose liberty might give them the animating hopes of recovering their own. All, bended beneath the yoke of Rome and her tyrants. 'Tis otherwise in modern times. Every country in Europe, where arbitrary power prevails, is surrounded by such as are free, which produces these different effects, it keeps ambitious men within bounds, and makes them afraid to proceed to extremities; it animates the minds of the people, and makes them hope to be what their neighbours are*; it spreads the principles of liberty over all Europe, and prevents the vital spark from being utterly extinguished in any country.

This might almost alone account for the unequal influence of the absolute power of the kings of France, and the Roman emperors, in

---

* Il est utile, qu'il-y ait un peuple libre, quand ce ne seroit que pour apprendre aux autres qu'ils peuvent l'être. *Mes Pensés.*

depressing genius and vitiating taste, even allowing them to have been equally despotic, which is far from being the case. All the states in Europe are so nicely ballanced, have so many interfering interests, and so much necessary communication with each other, that there is a sort of interchange of the opinions, principles and moral sentiments, as well as of the natural productions, and various manufactures of the different countries. In computing the freedom, the liberal spirit and taste, which may be supposed to prevail in any nation, we ought not only to take into the account the advantages, they derive from their own constitution, but likewise those which arise from their communication with other countries, and that protection which they may hope to find abroad, if they are oppressed at home. If we consider the circumstances of the French in these respects, we must certainly own, they are extremely favourable.

WITH

With this I shall conclude what I had to offer in anſwer to the objections, that may be brought againſt the happy influence of liberty upon taſte as well as genius, from what has happened in France in modern times. The natural influence of freedom to improve every faculty of the human mind, might indeed be proved by abſtract principles, but arguments of that ſort are always leſs entertaining than thoſe which are deduced from hiſtorical facts. Similar reaſonings and obſervations, made upon the circumſtances and ſituation of other nations, when your Lordſhip is reading the General Hiſtory of the world, may be ſucceſsfully employed to refute all the objections that can be brought againſt the principle, here attempted to be eſtabliſhed from the ſtate of taſte in any other country, even in modern Italy itſelf.

Your Lordſhip's genius will enable you to do this with much more advantage and pleaſure to yourſelf than I could do. The active exertion of one's own talents is always

more

more agreeable and improving, than tediously to follow the reasonings of another. But this puts me in mind that it is high time to conclude my letter, and to aſk pardon for having made it ſo long. I am,

My Lord, &c.

LETTER VIII.

Why POETRY has flourished more in England, than SCULPTURE or PAINTING.

MY LORD,

IF liberty, as I endeavoured to prove in some former letters, be favourable to genius and taste, and if Britain be the happy isle,

Where, long foretold, the people reigns;
Where each a vassal's humble heart disdains *;

* Dr. Akenside's ode to the earl of Huntingdon.

it may seem surprising that in some things we have been excelled, and in others so nearly equalled, by our less free neighbours. Can this be attributed to the genius of the people? It certainly cannot. That we have produced philosophers of superior merit, whose great efforts enabled them to attain to the highest pinnacle of the temple of wisdom, from whence they could behold those of other nations every where groping in the dark, and widely erring from the paths of truth and real science,* is undoubtedly certain: the awful name of Newton puts it beyond dispute. But, my Lord, it does more, it proves that this country must have produced geniuses, which, if properly encouraged, might have been capable of any thing. There is a natural connection between all the faculties of the human soul; an age and nation that produces great men in one way, might in

* ——Sapientum templa serena,
Despicere unde queas alios, passimque videre
Errare. ——————   *Lucret.*

another; if its genius were turned to that object. What power of the human mind can we suppose not to have been possessed by one, who could penetrate into the laws of nature, and unravel the amazing plan of the universe with such perspicuity as Sir Isaac Newton? Depth of judgment was not alone sufficient, the strongest *imagination* must have been necessary to enable one to conceive how the same force, which causes a stone to fall to the ground, makes the planets gravitate to each other, and to comprehend how the various laws of nature regulate the appearances and motions of those bodies, which the great Creator of all things hath exhibited to our view in the immensity of space! If Newton discovered less relish and taste for inferior beauties and harmonies, 'twas because his mind was occupied by a grander beauty, and a more divine harmony, that of the universe and the spheres. When men, eminent in that science in which he excelled, condescend to treat of inferior arts, they can convince the world how much they are capable of out-doing the rest of mankind even in these; a striking proof of which Dr. Smith has lately given in his Harmonics, a work, in which the true principles of music are allowed, by the best judges, to have been better explained than they ever were.

But not only in the sublime and philosophic sciences, even in arts which are allowed to depend more intimately upon the powers of imagination and a fine taste, Britain has produced such examples as may convince any one, that the inhabitants of this island, whenever they are properly encouraged, and apply to them, may excel in all the polite arts. Did the grand productions of Michael Angelo, in architecture, painting and statuary, require a greater sublimity of imagination than the Paradise Lost? Do the works of any landscape-painter discover a fancy more forcibly struck, or capable of describing natural objects with more truth or energy, than the *picturesque* pen of Thomson has done in his Seasons, a poem, which considered

sidered in this light is admirable, the ideas of almost every page of which, exhibited upon canvas, would, without any addition, make a striking landscape, equal perhaps to any of the most famous masters. Has not England produced writers of the comic kind of the greatest merit? We can indeed at present boast of a painter in this way, whose talents are unequalled and inimitable: Mr. Hogarth need not be named to let you know who this original genius is.

WHENCE then can it arise that, with a genius capable of excelling in all, the English have been eminent only in some particular branches of the fine arts, and that Britain has produced so many good poets, and no painters or statuaries capable of contending with Poussin, Le Brun, and Girardon? I do not mention these, as if I meant to say that they are the greatest masters in their different ways; I know the Raphaels; the Rubens, the Michael Angelos have greatly excelled them;

but

but I have named them, becaufe they are the boaft of a country that has fo long rivalled this ifland in every thing: but which the inhabitants of Great Britain have a genius capable of excelling, if proper encouragement was given to it, and proper methods taken to cultivate and improve it. This I fhall endeavour to illuftrate, and to offer fome reafons that may throw light upon the queftion, Why England has produced fo many great poets, and no capital painters or ftatuaries?

To anfwer the firft part of the queftion, one need only put another: why have the mufes had votaries in every country upon earth? Among barbarous and uncivilized nations, they have been worfhipped by rough unpolifhed bards, and in every polite and civilized country, by fuch as were infpired with a genius and tafte more fuitable to the dignity and elegance of thofe Deities? The firft writers almoft in every country were poets, one reafon of which may have been

been this: a sentiment, well expressed in harmonious verse, might perhaps never be so elegantly expressed again, even by the person who first uttered it; one word, nay the placing of a word, or the arrangement of a sentence, being forgot, the harmony is lost, and the pleasure we enjoyed, when listening to the sweet sounds, is felt no more. Hence those, whose genius enabled them to relate any adventure in elegant verse, or to sing of any subject in pleasing strains, conscious of the admiration with which they were heard, and afraid that these harmonious sentences should slip out of their memory, wrote them down, that they might have it in their power to please again with words, which they had found to please before. Emulation, and a desire of excelling, natural to man, prompted others to aspire to the same applause. As every country grew civilized, and its language elegant and correct, poets by degrees became more excellent, and their verses more polished and refined. 'Tis an entertaining speculation to reflect upon the gradual improvements

ments of nations and men; to trace the efforts of the British muse from the songs of the antient Druids to the sublime poetry of Milton, and the elegant and sensible verses of Pope.

Since knowledge and arts, forsaking the eastern regions of this globe, have deigned to visit the western world, Britain has been eminent for learning and science: its inhabitants have long vied with all their neighbours, and in latter ages have produced geniuses of such superior merit, as has rendered the victory in these articles, even in the opinion of the best judges among our rivals, immortal. Mr. Voltaire owns, that, if we consider the great and useful discoveries in philosophy, that age, which he esteems to have been the most enlightened of any, may with as much propriety be called the age of England, as of Lewis XIV*. Possessed too of a lan-

* C'est de son sein (la Societé Royale) que sortirent de nos jours les decouverts sur la lumiere, sur le principe

language originally copious and bold, and at last by many efforts highly improved, Britain has produced poets of a genius more resembling the noble spirit of the antients, than perhaps any other country in modern times. I say resembling the *spirit* of the antients, for it cannot be denied that their critical accuracy has been more copied by the writers of some other nations. To the genius of the people, and that elevated spirit which liberty inspires, we owe our excelling in the first: to our negligence, and to the superior care bestowed upon criticism in a neighbouring country, 'tis owing that we are excelled in the second.

It has often been observed, with a seeming depth of judgment, that academies and societies, established for the encouragement of

cipe de la gravitation, sur l'aberration des etoiles fixes, sur la geometrie transcendante, et cent autres inventions, qui pourraient a cet egard faire appeller ce siécle, le siécle des Anglois, aussi bien que celui de Louis XIV.

sciences and arts, for judging of the merit of works, and bestowing rewards and honors upon those who excel, in fact does more harm than good*. This observation, as it contradicts what appears to be at first evident, seems ingenious, but if we consider it, 'twill be found to be over-refined, and unjust. " In France, says Dr. Brown, the severities " of the academy have utterly quenched the " high tragic spirit †". However, this can hardly be allowed, when we reflect that even translations of Zara, and some other French tragedies of modern date, are favourite and stock-plays upon the English stage, and seem to be at least as spirited as several performances of our own tragic writers of the present times.

But though it were allowed that the high tragic spirit had utterly forsaken the French,

---

* Les academies, institues pour etendre le Genie, mais bien plus propres a le borner, ont fondé des prix, &c. *Mes Pensés.*

† Essays on the Characteristics, p. 34.

another and a better reason might be given for it; it might be supposed that the elevated spirit of tragedy would decay in a country where power has made such encroachments upon liberty. This would certainly have been the case, had not other favourable circumstances in some measure prevented it: among these, I cannot help being persuaded that the efforts of the academy ought not to be omitted, and that its institution may be said to be one reason, (besides those which I took notice of in a former letter) that has enabled the French to bear up against the mischievous influence of arbitrary power upon genius and taste.

If the natural effect of a gay and thoughtless court be to promote a taste for every thing that is frivolous and fantastical, and a relish for luxury and silly amusements, rather than manly pleasures and rational entertainments, can we conceive any thing better calculated to serve as an antidote against this relaxing poison, than the establishment of a society

society of men eminent for their parts, and among whom they alone can make a figure, who improve their talents and severely correct the irregularities of fancy and taste? If an admission into this society be aspired to as an honour by the greatest men of the country, both for abilities and rank, must it not naturally have this double effect? to excite every person of genius to endeavour to merit a place in it by cultivating his talents, and to render the society itself so respectable and illustrious, that its decisions will be regarded with veneration, and its taste, formed by a study of what is natural and just, and by being conversant with the sentiments of the greatest men both among the living and the dead, become so authoritative as even to be able to oppose that of a dissipated and unthinking court.

If in some countries, particularly in France, very small or perhaps no improvements have been made in the fine arts since the establishment of societies to promote and encourage them,

them, it muſt have proceeded from ſome circumſtances leſs friendly to genius and taſte than ſuch academies can poſſibly be ſuppoſed to be; or perhaps they had already been brought to the greateſt perfection the genius and language of the people were capable of. But without taking a great deal for granted, we may affirm, that, in all probability, had it not been for theſe inſtitutions, a decay of genius, and a corruption of taſte would have been both more real and apparent. Such ſocieties concurring with other favourable circumſtances can never be diſadvantageous. What was that aſſembly, in Greece, which at the feaſt of Minerva, diſtributed rewards and conferred honours upon the beſt poets, hiſtorians, and artiſts, but a ſociety of learned men, (for it conſiſted of a ſelect number) who, having improved their own talents, were capable of judging of the works of others, and of teaching the multitude to place their admiration upon worthy objects? Did not the honors, that were beſtowed upon Herodotus, fire the mind of

Thu-

Thucydides, then a boy, and prompt him to apply all the force of his genius to emulate or excel the father of History? Can we suppose that this institution had a bad effect, nay that it was not one of the principal causes of that genuine elegance and correctness of taste which rendered the works of Greece so inimitably beautiful?

If, indeed, such societies are not established 'till genius be visibly on the decline, they may be of little use. 'Tis too late to send a horse to the manage when his fire and vigour is gone, or after bad usage has broke his spirits; but certainly if he be taken while he yet *paweth in the valley and rejoiceth in his strength*, and sent to be trained in a proper manner, it will not be said that the skill of a master may not add a grace to all his motions, and correct the fury and irregularity of his unmanaged efforts, without making him a bit the less a spirited and noble animal. Care and study does not extinguish genius and fire, but makes them burn with a more equal and

and illuminating flame. Nothing can be better calculated to correct the irregular sallies of an ingenious people, and to reduce their compositions to a graceful form, than a society invested with dignity, and appointed to cultivate and promote the liberal arts. Had such a society been established in London, when Shakespear wrote, the works of that great man would not have afforded, " as Mr. Pope owns they do*, the most nu-" merous as well as most conspicuous in-" stances both of beauties and faults of all " sorts." The first indeed his genius would have abundantly supplied him with, but the last he would have been taught and encouraged to avoid, by having the countenance of good judges, and being supported against " the taste and humour that then prevail-" ed †".

Here then, we may perceive one reason why our neighbours with much less genius

* Preface to Shakespear.
† Id. et ibid.

have excelled us in correctness of taste. They have established in their metropolis, societies to superintend and direct the public approbation, while we have allowed the humours of the people to be the sovereign arbitrator. In dramatic performances, the Pit has always been able to condemn or approve, and this has generally been led by a few; who, without perhaps any other qualification but a larger share of briskness and conceit than the rest, have taken upon them to direct the judgment of the town. The universities, removed at a distance, could not have much influence: in these a foundation might be laid for excelling, by studying the originals of all beauty; but when works came to be offered to the town, 'twas found that a classical spirit was less calculated to please, than one more adapted to the taste of a place where no such learned societies were instituted, and where a different taste prevailed. Were a society, like the French academy, established in London, of such dignity as to make the most accomplished among the Great,

am-

ambitious of being members of it, it could not fail of having a happy influence. Not only would it serve to promote a good taste, it would also give a spur to genius, and encourage many people to cultivate talents, which at present they neglect. What an additional ornament would such a society be to the British metropolis! What an honor would be to its *Founder*, and to those whose interest and rank might give them an opportunity of promoting such an institution! This would make correctness of taste as much the characteristic of the English writers, as freedom and genius have hitherto been, and soon enable the British muses to become as superior to the French in the former as they are by all good judges allowed to be in the latter.

To the genius then of the people, and to that of liberty, to the boldness and copiousness of our language, we may ascribe the elevated spirit of British poetry; to the want of any learned societies, established in London, we may attribute those extravagant flights,

flights, and that irregularity, which, it muſt be owned, are too conſpicuous in ſome of the greateſt names among the Engliſh poets. But to what, my Lord, can it be aſcribed, that Britain has produced no painters or ſtatuaries, whoſe productions have been known beyond the limits of their own country; while Italy, the Low Countries, and France have produced maſters in that way, whoſe works have become precious over all the world, and for which immenſe ſums are every where given? This muſt ariſe from ſome cauſe or other in the circumſtances or genius of the people. I ſhall give you my conjectures about it: probability is all one can expect in ſuch a ſubject, though undoubtedly, in a nation ſo remarkable for genius in other reſpects as Great Britain has been, ſuch a deficiency muſt have ariſen from ſome fixed moral cauſes, and not from any accidental want of genius in that particular way.

When was it that England began to be eminent for a good taſte, and to boaſt of great poets? was it not about the time of
the

the reformation? An event in every other respect of the happiest consequence to this island, but which naturally gave a check to improvements in sculpture and painting, by taking away the greatest encouragements and motives to excel in these arts. In Italy, at the restoration of politeness and arts, poets and painters appeared at the same time.

A Raphael painted, and a Vida sung *.

In England, Spenser and Shakespear, much greater poets than Vida, were accompanied with no painters of any fame, much less able to enter the lists with Raphael the greatest master of his art, the modern world can boast of; and ever since the revival of letters and arts, Great Britain hath been left infinitely behind in painting by Italy, and other Roman Catholic countries, while our poets have sung with a nobler fire, and catched the free and manly spirit of the antients, more per-

* Pope's Essay on Criticism.

haps than has been done by those of any other country in modern times.

There are no passions of the human mind capable of being worked up to greater heights, or of producing stronger effects, than superstition and enthusiasm; hence we may easily conceive, what an influence the consecrating of statues and pictures, as objects of adoration in Roman Catholic countries, must have upon the minds of the people, and for what reasons no pains are spared, and no expence grudged, to procure pieces of the most striking beauty and expression to adorn popish altars, and to animate the devotion of superstitious votaries. Fact and experience, as well as reason and theory, confirm this opinion, and naturally account for those strong powers of fancy which Roman Catholic painters have discovered, and for that great encouragement they have met with from the *religious*. The first and the last works of almost all the great masters have been devotional pieces, and done too for some religious house.

Cim-

CIMABUE, the father and restorer of painting in modern times, when a boy, used to step from school and spend his hours in viewing those painters, which the governors of Florence had brought from Greece, and who were at work in the chapel of the family of Gondi, in the church of *Sancta Maria Novella* *. There he first had his imagination warmed, and formed those ideas of an art, he afterwards carried to a degree of perfection, which, though far inferior to what it has since arrived at, was infinitely superior to that in which he found it. A picture of the Blessed Virgin done by him for that very church was beheld with such admiration, that all the people of Florence went to receive it from him at his house, and conducted it with extraordinary demonstrations of joy, with great pomp and the sound of trumpets, to the church where it was to be placed †. Such honors must have power-

---

* Felib. Vies de Peint.

† Les ouvrages qu'il fit parurent si admirables en comparison des autres qu'on voyoit en ce tems la, qu'ayant

powerfully incited others to endeavour to excel in an art that could acquire one so much applause.

THE History of the most famous modern painters is principally taken up with accounts of the encouragement they received from Popes, and of the pictures they did for churches and religious houses *. Raphael was so highly honoured by Julius II. and Leo X. that he even hoped to have been made a Cardinal †. His greatest and best pieces were done for churches, and the subjects of them are taken from sacred history. The Transfiguration, his last and most perfect performance, shews how much his imagination was elevated above vulgar conceptions by a study of the sublime passages of Scripture, since he has

---

ayant peint un vierge pour metre dans l'Eglise de Santa Maria Novella de Florence, tout le peuple fut prendre ce tableau chez lui, et avec une joye extraordinaire, le porta en pomp, au bruit de trompettes, jusq'au lieu ou il devoit être posé.   Felib. Vies de Peint.

* Felib. Vies des Peint. passim.   † Id.

given

given such a divine resplendence to the figure of our Saviour, as is allowed to be indeed wonderful, and makes a fine writer say, that he exerted a last and great effort, to shew the power of his art, in conveying an idea even of things which are inexpressible*. But 'tis unnecessary to shew what motives to excel, and how much employment the image worship of the church of Rome gives to painters and statuaries; this is so evident as to stand in need of no illustration. I shall only add, that the fine pictures and statues, with which the Popish altars are adorned, and to which their religion commands the people to fix their eyes with devout attention, must give an opportunity of viewing fine pieces, and of having one's fancy often warmly struck with the charming productions of sculpture and painting, which is not to be met with in Protestant countries, and consequently must afford young people many occasions of

---

* Il a fait un dernier effort, pour montrer la puissance de son art dans les choses même qui ne se peuvent exprimer.   Felib. Vies des Peint.

feeling

feeling the power of their genius, and of discovering their taste for the imitative arts. Besides, a picture, which devotion bids one behold with veneration, must make a far deeper impression upon the mind, and affect it with a more sensible rapture, than it could possibly do, were one only to look at it as a common piece of art, or from no other motive but to gratify taste or curiosity. Strange things have been told of the strong impressions made by images upon the imagination, and of the effect of such impressions. The ingenious Malbranche tells us, I think, for I have not got his book by me, of a woman who bore a child with a face exactly resembling the image of an old Saint, to which she had constantly paid her devotions during the time of her pregnancy. If this story be true, it is a striking proof with what sensibility pictures are sometimes beheld by those who kneel to popish shrines. And if the theory, that every sentiment of the mother is in some measure communicated to the foetus, be just, it proves too, that the

im-

impression, made by a picture upon the fancy of the mother, must in a small degree affect the child's, and stamp an original taste for painting upon its imagination. Thus the circumstances that are favourable to the arts of painting and sculpture in Roman-catholic countries may be traced back even to the most distant and primitive impressions that are stamped upon the human mind.

HERE, however, I cannot help taking notice that, though it must be owned that the sensible objects, which are consecrated by the church of Rome to excite the devotion of the people, give a superior advantage to countries, where that religion prevails, to excel in the plastic arts, 'tis no argument for us to fall in love with popery, or to become less zealous against its superstition. The productions of painting and sculpture have often been made use of by designing men to work up devotion to wild enthusiasm, and a reverence for the supreme Being to abject and cruel superstition. Besides, the rapture, which one feels, when

when viewing exquisite pieces of art, attaches the mind almost wholly to sensible objects, and obscures those intellectual conceptions of the divinity, which are alone proper, especially when we approach to worship the father of the universe, who is a spirit, and must be worshipped in spirit. Struck with the visible image, the mind forgets the invisible Being, and like Æmilius when he beheld the Jupiter of Phidias, is apt to imagine that it sees Jove himself*.

I cannot help being persuaded that the situation of Great Britain has been another reason why sculpture and painting have made so small progress in this country. Living in an island, and almost separated from the rest of the world, the inhabitants of England have been less visited by foreigners of *distinction* than those of any other part of Europe of equal consequence, and thus have wanted one motive to encourage arts that are

* Jovem velut præsentem. *Liv.* see above, page 116.

ornamental, the vanity of difplaying grand works to ftrangers. The ftates on the Continent, being as it were thorough-fares to each other, and often viewed not only by foreigners who come to refide in them, but by thofe who pafs through them in their way to neighbouring countries, have been incited by a natural defire of making their country look fine in the eyes of ftrangers, to cultivate thofe arts, which have always been allowed to conduce moft to the ornament and embellifhment of a nation; architecture, fculpture, and painting. To what other caufe can we afcribe it, that the chief towns of fome fmall ftates abroad have more public ornaments than this great and opulent city? In modern times indeed the number of foreigners who live and do bufinefs in London is immenfe, but even now we are perhaps lefs vifited out of curiofity, and by people of fafhion who travel for improvement *alone*, than any other confiderable nation in Europe, certainly much lefs fo than moft of them.

But

But whether the want of that emulation, which is naturally excited by being visited by ingenious foreigners and people of distinction has been one cause or not why the plastic arts have been little cultivated here, what I am going to mention will certainly be owned to have been a principal reason of it. The English nobility and people of fashion have resided less in London, than those of the same rank in other nations have done in the capitals of their different countries. I shall not enter into the dispute how far this may have been of advantage to the kingdom in general, or what bad effects may arise from the taste for living in town, or near it, that has of late prevailed so much among people of rank and fortune beyond what it did in former times: whatever bad consequences may flow from this humour in other respects, it must be allowed to have a natural tendency to improve and polish the manners of the people, to promote a taste for what is elegant and splendid, and to afford the greatest encouragement and opportunities to cultivate

tivate the fine arts. The truth of this observation may be proved from reason as well as from experience. In every nation, that has made a figure for politeness, the capital has been the principal residence of all who have been eminent for the accomplishments of their minds, and the elegance of their tastes. How, indeed, should it be otherwise? Man is a social creature: there is a natural and strong attraction, by which those of similar characters and pursuits are drawn together. 'Tis not in every village or country-neighbourhood, that one, who has been well educated, and taken care to improve his talents, can meet with many who are able to gratify that desire, which all have of contracting friendships with persons whose knowledge and sentiments are upon a level with their own.

HENCE men become desirous of living in capitals and populous cities, where the largeness and extent of society gives the greater chance of meeting with persons of a turn of mind suited and agreeable to their own. It is altogether unneceſſary to endeavour to prove how much ſociety and the converſation of ſenſible and ingenious men correct every error and improve every talent of the human mind. This is felt and acknowledged by every one capable of improvement, but by none more than by thoſe, who have a taſte for the fine arts. In the retired ſhades of a college, abſtract ſcience and profound learning may flouriſh more than in the gay ſunſhine of a brilliant metropolis; but 'tis not ſo with the imitative arts, particularly ſculpture and painting. 'Tis among the ruins of the large cities of antiquity, that the precious remains of ancient art are to be found. Nor will theſe arts ever be greatly improved in any country, 'till a taſte for embelliſhing the metropolis ariſes, and a truly elegant one can never ariſe 'till thoſe of rank and fortune reſide ſome part of the year in the capital. A nobleman, who lives generally in the country, may ſpend a great deal of money in adorning his country-ſeat, but after he has done

done all that he possibly can to make it grand as well as elegant, it will not have so sensible an effect to diffuse a good taste, as a house built (at much less expence) in a city would have. In towns every thing is criticised, and approved or condemned, the number of artists, their taste and their emulation, the multitude of spectators, indeed every circumstance contributes to inspire those, who are to execute any piece of work, that is to be exposed to the eyes of the public, to do all they can to correct their designs, avoid censure, and merit the approbation of good judges. On the other hand, fine works, by being exposed to the view of many, have a considerable influence to give just ideas of what is beautiful or grand.

But not only does this improve artists themselves: they who employ them receive much improvement, and are taught what is really elegant, and what is not so. Whatever a nobleman does in a remote part of the country is admired and praised by those around

around him: in cities this does not happen. Thofe who are upon a level with the Great, or independent, will not fcruple to find fault with their tafte. Men are afhamed of being thought vulgar or unpolifhed in any thing; hence the natural effect of people of fafhion's living in town is, that both the external appearance of their houfes, and the ornaments within, are gradually improved and become elegant and fine: pictures and ftatues, as the nobleft embellifhments, become almoft neceffary to every houfe of tafte: great encouragement is given to the art of painting, and this promotes emulation among the profeffors of that art, the neceffary confequence of which is improvement and fkill.

THIS reafoning is certainly juft, but a view of what actually has happened greatly confirms it.

SINCE London became the general refidence of people of rank for a confiderable part of the year, what improvements have
   been

been made, and are daily making! To name particulars is unneceſſary; they are known to every one, and I am perſuaded that in a few years this metropolis will be as famous for its elegant buildings, and for artiſts that excel in painting and ſculpture, as it is at preſent for its opulence and trade. The encouragement, that hath been lately given to theſe arts, has already had a ſenſible effect, and will in time convince the world, that it was not owing to any want of genius, but to other circumſtances, that the Engliſh have excelled leſs in ſculpture and painting than in poetry. Succeſsful in war, and ſuperior to our rivals in arms, many favourable circumſtances give us the beſt grounds to hope, that we ſhall ſoon be equally ſo in every other reſpect. While their ſpirits are depreſſed, ours muſt riſe: while their government, chagrined with repeated diſappointments, will in all probability grow more ſevere; we have the happy proſpect of ſeeing religion, virtue, liberty, ſcience and arts encouraged and flouriſhing amongſt us. In-
ſpired

spired by Royal Example, those of distinguished rank, will be incited to promote every thing that tends to the good, the honour, and the improvement of their country. The spirit of the times in which your Lordship has the happiness to be called upon to act your part in life, will be an additional motive to prompt you to do it in that noble and generous manner which so much becomes your high rank, and is so agreeable to your natural taste and good dispositions.

I am,

My Lord, &c.

FINIS.

ERRATA.

Page 61. l. 15. for *spend*, read *spent*.
119. l. 2. for *study that*, read *study of that*.
159. l. 8. for *fields*, read *field*.
173. l. 19. after *liberty*, put a ;
191.   for *Maupertius*, read *Maupertuis*.
192. l. 6. for *l'aime*, read *l'ame*.
206. l. 4. for *does*, read *do*.

www.ingramcontent.com/pod-product-compliance
Lightning Source LLC
Chambersburg PA
CBHW021808230426
43669CB00008B/670